Algorithms and Data Structures in Computer Engineering

Computer Science Publishing Program

ALGORITHMS and DATA STRUCTURES in COMPUTER ENGINEERING

E. STEWART LEE
Computer Systems Research Institute
University of Toronto
Toronto, Ontario

JONES AND BARTLETT PUBLISHERS
BOSTON   LONDON

Editorial, Sales, and Customer Service Offices
Jones and Bartlett Publishers
One Exeter Plaza
Boston, MA 02116
617-859-3900
1-800-832-0034

Jones and Bartlett Publishers International
P O Box 1498
London W6 7RS
England

Library of Congress Cataloging-in-Publication Data

Lee, E. Stewart.
    Algorithms and data structures in computer engineering / E. Stewart Lee.
        p.   cm.
    Includes bibliographical references (p. 211) and index.
    ISBN 0-86720-219-X
    1. Computer algorithms.   2. Data structures (Computer science)
3. Computer engineering.   I. Title.
QA76.9.A43L44   1991
005.7'3—dc20   91-82356
                                                            CIP

Printed in the United States of America
96 95 94 93   10 9 8 7 6 5 4 3 2

TABLE OF CONTENTS

Contents

PREFACE

The successful use of computers is crucial in effective engineering practice. The modern discipline of computer engineering embodies the knowledge necessary to use computers properly and constructively. Lurking under this discipline of computer engineering is the craft of programming. This course is about the fundamentals of the software side of computer engineering as a scientific discipline. The course is also about its requisite partner, the craft of programming. Without programming, the engineering of software becomes an esoteric exercise in science, with little thought of the practicalities attendant on actually making it go. The art of actually making it go is the essence of engineering.

Programming is strongly affected by the scale of the problem. Large or complicated problems involve a methodology of thought that must be both systematic and scientific. This methodology is not obvious, but it can be demonstrated even if small problems are the vehicle used to illustrate it.

In common with many other engineering activities, a good program begins with a good plan. Programming is a skilled occupation. It can be thought of as an art. It is not something that can be learned by poring over books. Consequently, any useful course in programming will have a laboratory. And it must be a laboratory, not a tutorial or a set of take-home problems. In programming, one can easily be overwhelmed by the volume of detail that must be considered. Often, there are great repercussions behind some of the detail. The mere presentation of an algorithm's principle and its mathematical analysis may be stimulating and challenging to the academic mind, but programs must be written in order for the lessons to sink in.

The first part of the course starts with a discussion of the methodology used to create good programs. The second topic in the course is the analysis of algorithms. The mathematical determination of the expected performance of an algorithm serves to introduce this subject. Examples of actual problems, somewhat simplified to expose the principles without shrouding them in irrelevant detail, are used as a vehicle to discuss this analysis. This leads to a brief exposure to some of the elementary notions of computational complexity. The goal here is to exhibit the importance of analysis in software engineering.

Recursion is the third topic in the course. One of the cornerstones of algorithm design is recursion. It can reduce the complicated to the elegant and the elaborate to the simple. It is, consequently, no surprise that recursion is central to the conception of many algorithms. Recursion is an important and powerful concept in programming. Recursion sometimes allows for an elegant, natural representation of a solution.

Programs that engineers must write will include all aspects of data structuring. The algorithms embodied in the program manipulate the data. The data structures and the algorithms must be designed as a unit. Doing otherwise is as absurd as trying to conceive the rules of a board game, without considering the layout of the board or the permitted movements of the pieces. If a rigid data structure is given, little flexibility remains in the choice of an efficient algorithm. When the structure of the data is part of the engineering problem, the designer has an unusual opportunity that he must be equipped to capitalize on.

This is not a beginning course in programming. Introductory courses have illustrated the principles of coding a program and getting a computer to respond to it in a satisfactory way. However, introductory programming courses concentrate on elementary algorithms. Usually, precious little structured data is encountered, and then only in a notational way that hides the implications of the structure. In practice, it is often the case that a data structure changes during the execution of the program. The structure of data is not always static. It will retain its basic properties, but will progress through a number of structural stages with the operation of the algorithm that manipulates it. Data structures that change during execution are the fourth topic in the course. Data structures that are defined in terms of themselves, called recursive data structures, are the most significant part of this topic. In particular, binary tree structures are studied extensively. Hash tables, which are often preferred to search trees, are also included.

Many programming problems are inherently hard, in the sense that they take so long to solve that approximations or partial solutions must be resorted to. An example of this kind of problem is exhaustive search. An introduction to this problem is the fifth topic in the course.

The second part of the course is a large example of the application of algorithms and data structures to a practical, interesting problem. This is introduced starting with the sixth topic. This topic consists of a concise introduction to formal language definition and structure. Several features of languages are considered to determine their impact on the properties of actual programming languages. This is a much more practical way to compare languages than the more superficial differences of their detailed syntax. Few courses at the second-year level include this material, it is central to the understanding of the fundamental distinctions between programming languages.

Probably the most important tool that a computer engineer uses, at least for software work, is the compiler that translates his programs into machine language. As an extension to the study of formal languages, and as an example of a non-trivial algorithm, a model of the nature of a compiler is examined. The definition of formal languages and the problem of parsing is introduced. This material is rarely found in a course at this level. However, it is important that a fairly large, interesting, and pertinent algorithm be examined. What could be better than to combine this desire with an introduction to how a compiler is engineered? Another reason for including this material is that all engineers who aspire to be effective programmers should have some insight into the basic techniques used in compilers.

A course that includes programming is often identified with the programming language used to implement the laboratory assignments. This is a mistake. Courses for artisans should not be identified by the tools they use. What is wanted is a language that will permit the illumination of the art, without obscuring the underlying lessons. The language also must be convenient to use and preferably have a compiler that runs efficiently and provides useful diagnostics. There are several suitable vehicles for doing this. Instead of recommending one practical language, these notes use a simple, generic language that should be immediately obvious to anyone who has mastered any procedural language. The programming examples in the text are presented in this language.

This book has grown from notes that were prepared for a course that was taught to engineering science students at the University of Toronto, starting in 1966 and intensifying in the early 1970's. Later, in the 1980's, the course evolved and the students came to include electrical engineers and computer engineers as well as engineering scientists. The notes were updated each year to reflect the changing discipline as well as to include material suitable for the new students who were to take the course. Many of these students have helped develop this book. Additionally, Tamara Hayes and Bob Soper have made many useful suggestions. Both were supervising tutors working with this material. Jack Gorrie identified numerous parts of the notes that were less than adequate. He has been a great help.

1 MAINTAINABLE AND TRUSTWORTHY SOFTWARE

1.1. INTRODUCTION

One of the interesting differences between software engineering and most other branches of engineering is the importance of design in normal day-to-day activities. All engineers do some design, but most design problems are rigidly circumscribed by the available technology, componentry, or practices. An electrical engineer designing some computer peripheral device will have to conform to the physical and electrical standards that the computer designers established. A mechanical engineer designing some complicated part that will be assembled with the assistance of robots will be often quite limited by the need to conform to the capabilities of the robots. Often the real problem is not the design of the unit itself, but the myriad problems that can occur due to this requirement for conformance.

Software engineers do not seem to be nearly so constrained by the ability of the computer system to do the job. Most software projects involve a major design component, and if this design is done poorly the result will be an unsatisfactory program. Sound engineering practice will produce a program design that solves the right problem. Sound programming practice will transform that design into a program that works reliably, is easy to use, and is unlikely to operate in a mischievous or absurd way. In common with many other engineering activities, a good program begins with a good design. Engineers have evolved a successful approach to design. This chapter is about that approach.

1.2. THE GOALS OF SOFTWARE DESIGN

This chapter presents a method for writing computer programs in a way that attacks these problems according to the following criteria:

Maintainability and Portability

Software is not static. New and attractive hardware is continually being announced. It is highly desirable that the evolution of new versions of existing systems, whether on the same or different equipment, be a practical process.

Trustworthiness

Computer programs must be worthy of trust. In far too many cases the part of a proposed system involving computer software is suspect from the beginning, and the ultimate performance of the software all too often confirms these suspicions.

1.2.1. Program Trustworthiness

A good program must be simple, reliable and adaptable. Without simplicity, one cannot expect to understand the purpose and details of a large program. Without reliability, one cannot seriously depend on it. Without adaptability to changing requirements, a program eventually becomes a fossil.

Fortunately, these essential requirements go hand in hand. Simplicity gives one the confidence to believe that a program works and makes it clear how it can be changed. Simplicity, reliability, and adaptability make a program manageable.

In addition, it is desirable to create programs that can work efficiently on several different computers for a variety of similar applications. This implies a need for efficiency, portability, and generality. But efficiency, portability, and generality should never be sought at the expense of simplicity, reliability, and adaptability, for only the latter qualities make it possible to understand what programs do, to depend on them, and to extend their capabilities.

The poor quality of much existing software is, to a large extent, the result of turning these priorities upside down. Some programmers justify extremely complex and incomprehensible programs by their high efficiency. Others claim that the poor reliability and efficiency of their huge programs are outweighed by their broad scope of application. The efficiency of a tool that nobody fully understands seems irrelevant. It is difficult to appreciate a general-purpose tool that is so slow that it cannot do anything well. It is self-evident that whenever program qualities appear to be in conflict with one another, the issue should consistently be settled by giving first priority to manageability, second priority to efficiency, and third priority to generality. This boils down to the two simple rules of

(1)   developing the program only after the problem is fully understood, and

(2)   limiting our range to those problems that the available tools can handle well.

Although this is too narrow a view for experimental computer usage, it is the only sound approach for professional programming.

1.2.2. Simplicity

Often, it is necessary to write programs that are so large that one cannot understand them all at once. We must reason about them in smaller pieces. Ideally, these pieces should be so small that any one of them is trivial to understand in itself. It would be best if they were no more than one page of text each so that they could be comprehended at a glance. Such a program could be studied page by page as one studies the maps in an atlas. In the end, when we have understood what all the pieces do, we must still be able to see what their combined effect as a whole is. If it is a program of many pages we can only do this by ignoring most of our detailed knowledge about the pieces and relying on a much simpler description of what they do and how they work together. An atlas can be as detailed as required, but one must realize that everything shown in the atlas is not available on any practical globe. Thus our program pieces must allow us to separate their detailed behavior from that small part of it that is of interest when we consider combinations of such pieces. In other words, we must distinguish between the inner and outer behavior of a program piece.

Program pieces must be built to perform well-defined, simple functions. These are then combined into large configurations to carry out more complicated functions. These aggregations are called subprograms or modules in our list of tools. This design method is effective because it splits a complicated task into simpler ones. First you convince yourself that the pieces work individually, and then you think about how they work together. During the second part of the argument, it is essential to be able to forget how a piece works in detail; otherwise, the problem becomes too complicated. In doing so, however, one makes the fundamental assumption that a piece always will do the same thing when it carries out its function.

Reproducible behavior is therefore a vital property of the program pieces that we need in order to build larger programs. We must keep this in mind when we select the kind of program pieces that will make up large programs. In many of the programs of interest, asynchronous events will take place at rates not fully controlled by the programmer. They depend on the environment in which the problem exists, which will often include direct connections to the *real world*. This means that a conscious effort must be made to design programs with reproducible behavior.

The idea of reasoning first about what a piece does, and then studying how it does it, is most effective if we can repeat this process by explaining each piece in terms of simpler pieces that themselves are built from still simpler pieces. Thus we shall confine ourselves to hierarchical structures composed of layers of program pieces.

Programs written in high-level languages are unable to modify themselves. They still have broad interfaces in the form of global variables that can be changed by every statement (by intention or mistake). Uncontrolled intercommunication through such mechanisms is totally contrary to the requirements of simplicity, understandability, reliability, adaptability, trustworthiness, and maintainability. It is necessary to control the access to non-local variables in a way that is consistent with these notions.

The main contribution to simplicity of a good programming language is to provide an abstract readable notation that makes the parts and structure of programs obvious to a reader. An abstract programming language suppresses machine detail such as addresses, registers, bit patterns, interrupts, and sometimes even the number of processors available. An ordinary programmer must not and should not be permitted to deal directly with absolute machine addresses. Instead the language must rely on abstract concepts such as variables and data types. As a result, program texts written in abstract languages are often an order of magnitude shorter than those written in machine language. This textual reduction simplifies program engineering considerably.

1.2.3. Reliability

Even the most readable language notation cannot prevent programmers from making mistakes. Programmers are, after all, normally human. In looking for these mistakes in large programs we need all the help we can get. The objective is to build up our level of confidence that the program does what it should do, no more and no less. There is a whole range of available techniques: correctness proofs, verification, proofreading, compilation checks, execution checks, and systematic testing. With the exception of correctness proofs, all these techniques play an important part in our technique.

Mathematically based correctness proofs are not practical for programs of commercial size, since they are still at an experimental stage. Since our aim is to describe techniques that are immediately useful for professional software development, they will not be discussed further.

Verification is the demonstration that several representations of the desired calculation agree at the same stage of progress of the computation. Among the useful verification techniques, those that reveal errors at the earliest possible time during program development are emphasized. The ability to assert conditions that must be true at various stages of execution of a program is a valuable verification tool. The compiler checks what it can check, and produces object text to do the rest.

One of the features of any good compiler is to push the role of compilation checks to the limit and reduce the use of execution checks as much as possible. This is not done just to make compiled programs more efficient by reducing the overhead of execution checks. In program engineering, compilation checks and execution checks play the same role as preventive maintenance and flight recorders do in aviation. The latter only tells you why a system crashed; the former helps prevent it. This distinction seems essential in the design of real-time systems that will control vital functions, such as nuclear plants or medical equipment. Such systems must be highly reliable before they are put into operation.

Extensive compilation checks are possible only if the language notation is redundant. The programmer must be able to specify important properties in several different ways so that a compiler can look for inconsistencies. An example is the use of declarations to introduce variables and their types before they are used in statements. The compiler could easily derive this information from the statements, provided these statements were always correct.

Testing can be used only to show the presence of errors but never their absence. However, it seems valuable to show the presence of errors and remove them one at a time. The combination of proper specification and design and documentation, followed by careful proofreading, extensive compilation checks, and systematic testing is an effective way to make a program so dependable that it can work without problems for an arbitrarily long time. That is about as reliable as any technology can be expected to be.

Program testing is often considered difficult because the addition of a new program piece can spread a burst of errors throughout the rest of a program and make previously tested pieces behave differently. This clearly violates the sound principle of being able to assume that when you have built and tested a part of a large program it will continue to behave correctly under all circumstances. Modern programming languages include tools (modules) that facilitate the sealing off of previously proven pieces, so that they cannot go awry.

1.2.4. Adaptability and Portability

A large program is so expensive to develop that it must be used for several years to make the effort worthwhile. As time passes the users' needs change, and it becomes necessary to modify the program to satisfy them. Quite often these modifications are done by people who did not develop the program in the first place. Their main difficulty is to find out how the program works and whether it will still work after being changed.

A small group of people can often succeed in developing the first version of a program in a low-level language with little or no documentation to support them. They do it by talking to one another daily and by sharing a mental picture of a simple structure. Later, when the same program must be extended by other programmers who are not in frequent contact with the original designers, it becomes painfully clear that the "simple" structure is not described anywhere and certainly is not revealed by the primitive language notation used. It is important to realize that for program maintenance a simple and well-documented structure is vital.

The ability to use the same program on a variety of computers is desirable for both technical and economic reasons. Many users have different computers. Sometimes they replace computers with newer ones. Quite often they need to use programs developed on other machines. Portability is only practical if programs are written in abstract languages that hide the differences between computers as much as possible.

1.2.5. Efficiency

Efficient programs save time for people waiting for results and reduce the cost of computation. While there are many dodges that purport to introduce efficiency, ultimately a compiler's ability to emit good, efficient code is essential. Stated another way, the efficiency of the programmer's code is strongly affected by the quality of the code emitted by the compiler. A good workman uses good tools. That is one of the reasons why organizations normally standardize on a few programming languages and compilers.

1.2.6. Generality

The use of the kind of language being described here no doubt reduces the range of applications that can be effectively tackled. The imposition of structure is equivalent to the imposition of restrictions on freedom of programming. One cannot use the machine in any way one wants, because the language makes it impossible to talk directly about some machine features. One cannot delay certain program decisions until execution time, because the compiler checks and freezes things much earlier. The freedom one loses is often illusory anyhow, since it can complicate programming to the point where simplicity and reliability and adaptability are lost.

1.3. ENGINEERING A GOOD PROGRAM

The engineering of a good program follows a number of proven steps, regardless of the size of the effort involved. Some programs, like those that will be written in this course, are basically one-person efforts, requiring a limited expenditure of time and concentrating on a single understood problem. Other programs require a much larger effort. Some operating systems have taken several years of effort by hundreds of programmers to produce the first version. Other programs have taken even longer to produce.

In principle, the steps that should be followed in producing a program are the same, whether the program is expected to have 100 lines of code or to be many thousands of times larger. There is, of course, a big difference between one or two people and a huge team of workers developing a program. The problems that are encountered with the team are all the ones that occur with the smaller effort, plus all the problems of scale associated with management, communications, quality control, enforcement of standards, and decision making. The methods used to overcome these problems of scale are a study in themselves. In this course, it is natural and sensible to concentrate on the smaller effort.

There are a number of definite steps that can be taken to help ensure that the program design process will lead to a satisfactory result. Following these steps in an intelligent way is nearly certain to guarantee a program that solves the right problem, that is robust and trustworthy, and that is maintainable. Figure 1.1 shows these steps in a way that is intended to indicate the progression of activity that should be undertaken when writing a program. The following sections describe each of these activities.

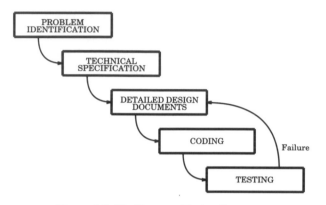

Figure 1.1: The Program Design Process.

1.3.1. Problem Identification

The first step in any programming design is to identify the problem that is being solved, to write down the range of values that the input variables and parameters can have, to establish the error conditions that could occur in the inputs and in the solution and what to do about them, and generally to comprehend the specification of what it is that is desired as a solution.

Another activity that should be a part of this step is to specify the tests that the program will eventually be required to handle satisfactorily in order to be said to work. Designing these tests involves careful planning. Error conditions should each be tested, and multiple errors should be thought about. The extreme values of input data and parameters should be tested to ensure that the program will work over the range required. Some representative typical input data should be included in the tests, even though the results of the program may not be known except for special values of the input data. Occasionally it is very difficult to contrive realistic test cases, but somehow at least a few must be generated.

The problem identification's purpose is to ensure that the program will solve the problem that it is desired to solve and not some closely related problem. After this step is taken the designer should present its results to his client or employer and ask for agreement that a program that behaves as specified will be satisfactory.

1.3.2. Technical Specification

The problem identification has resulted in a description of the problem as the user sees it. The technical specification is a version of the same material written from the point of view of the software engineer who must write the program. It will specify the same things from a technical point of view. Such things as mathematical methods, data structures, and the details of output formats will be a part of this specification. It will also describe the overall structure of the program and identify the modules and subprograms that will be a part of the solution.

Engineers have traditionally used technical drawing to describe a design they are making. The technical specification document is analogous to the assembly drawings, sectional views, and other drawings that show the complete design and the way the various parts of the design fit together.

1.3.3. Detailed Design Documents

Working from the technical specification, the details of each subcomponent are fully documented. The documentation should show the input data, parameters, and output results of the subcomponent, what it does, and how it is to do it. Each detailed design document should be sufficient so that a programmer can implement the subcomponent with little knowledge of the rest of the program. Following the analogy of engineering drawing, these documents correspond to the detailed engineering drawings of each part that might be given to a machine shop or a subcontractor for manufacturing purposes.

At this stage in the process, no program has been written that will become a part of the final product. The design has concentrated on documentation. It is evident, however, that the intellectual problems associated with the design will have been solved, and the remaining steps are somewhat mundane and automatic.

1.3.4. Coding

Working from the technical specification and the detailed design documentation, a program is coded following the documentation already done. If some problem erupts during this step that was not anticipated during the earlier stages, coding should be halted while the documentation is modified and then resumed according to the new documentation. It is often more productive to discard large parts of the code already written rather than to make an attempt to rescue code that conforms to the earlier specification.

When the code is complete, it is compiled and the inevitable crop of typographical and other syntactical blunders corrected. When this has been completed, there will be a very good chance that the program will work properly.

1.3.4.1. Program Subcomponents

Breaking up the coding into pieces, each described by one of the detailed design documents, is logical. This brings up the use of subprograms and modules.

A subprogram — a procedure or a function — is a functional unit that it is convenient and sensible to code independently from the rest of the program. In the smaller program, the desired subdivision of the programming effort can be obtained with procedures and functions alone. If the program has only a few hundred lines of code, procedures and functions are almost always sufficient. In this case, particularly if the program is implemented by one person, the use of visibility controls (modules with imports and exports) may be overkill.

A *module* is a self-contained program component with an explicit interface to the outside world. The module's exports list determines how much of its internals is visible to the user of the module. The imports list specifies which externally defined modules, routines, and data structures it requires. Combined with a description of the module's function, these import and export lists are sufficient information to permit the module's use. Implementation details internal to the module, such as the specifications of unexported data structures and routines, are guaranteed by the compiler to be invisible to users of the module. This invisibility is important because it means that no hidden dependencies may exist between modules and that two modules with identical interfaces (though differing substantially in their internal implementation) may be freely interchanged.

The use of modules is an effective programming practice for larger programs. The module's internal routines may manipulate various sets of data, but together they implement some discernible functional block within the program.

1.3.4.2. Parameterization

There may be type, variable, and constant definitions associated with the program. These in effect parameterize the program by specializing each new compiled instance of the program. Examples of program parameters are table sizes, maximum message lengths, and named constants. Such program parameters should be collected together in one place, preferably toward the beginning of the program where they can be found easily. Pertinent comments should indicate what the parameter is and what effect changing it will have. If modules are used, each might have its own collection of parameters to augment those of the main program.

1.3.4.3. Assertions

An *assertion* is a programmer-supplied logical-valued expression representing a condition or program state that must hold if the program is correct. Assertions may appear almost anywhere a statement can appear. An assertion embedded in a sequence of executable statements is evaluated whenever execution reaches the assert statement. Assertions within the declaration sections of modules are evaluated as the module is initialized before program execution. Failure of an assertion causes the immediate termination of execution.

Assertions are used to check the validity of routine parameters, the consistency of program or module data, and the progress of computation. *Assertion of computational progress* is a vague-sounding phrase but an important one. It means that at various points in the body of a routine a programmer may assert that some desired computational state has been achieved. These assertions unambiguously express the programmer's understanding of the program's operation and the intended effect of each sequence of statements. In this way, assertions resemble embedded program documentation. The great advantage of assertions over comments for this purpose is that the validity of an assertion is checkable during execution.

Assertions should only be used to state conditions that the programmer believes will always hold. That is, the failure of an assertion should always imply a logic or programming error. Errors such as table overflows and invalidity of data read from a terminal are under the control of the end user rather than the programmer and are to be explicitly detected and handled in some appropriate, less drastic way.

1.3.5. Testing

The tests that were conceived in the first step are now tried. If the steps have been followed properly, they should work without difficulties. If they do not work properly, the problem may be that the coding was incorrect. It can be changed and the tests retried.

In the event that a serious problem occurs, changing the code without changing the design documents is a recipe for wasting time.

Bite the bullet, go back and change the design, then the code, and the problem will most likely clear up much more rapidly.

Two things are certain:

(1)   Running exactly the same test again, without any changes, will produce exactly the same result.

(2)   Cosmetic changes to the program, not based on thought but rather on a belief in random chance, are doubly disastrous.

Cosmetic changes to a program transform the code away from the design, so that it is likely that the program no longer has a close relation to the problem, and they tend to persist in the code with unfortunate results later when the real problem is discovered.

The steps described above have been evolved over many years of practice. They work. Use them, and you will find that your productivity will improve dramatically.

2 THE COMPLEXITY OF ALGORITHMS

2.1. INTRODUCTION

It is intuitive that some ways of calculating things are better than other ways. The study of various measures to characterize the properties of algorithms, both to compare several different computational techniques, and to provide an absolute measure of how much time or space will be required to solve some problem, is the study of the complexity of algorithms.

2.2. TIME COMPLEXITY

In practice algorithms that deal with a fixed number of data objects are of little interest from a complexity point of view. They take a certain time to run, and that is that. A more interesting case is when the number of data objects may change with different executions of the algorithm. The variation of the execution time of the algorithm as a function of the number of data objects is known as the complexity of the algorithm.

Suppose there are n objects, and suppose by a suitable analysis it is known that the algorithm takes $T(n)$ seconds to run. Usually, $T(n)$ is not known in absolute terms. That would require a knowledge of the running time of all of the instructions in the machine, and perhaps of the operating system as well. Usually, $T(n)$ can be found to within the value of one or more unknown constants. These constants are unknown because the actual time that the instructions will take on the machine that will execute the algorithm is not necessarily known. In fact, the actual machine may be unknown. What is desired is a *relative* measure of the complexity of the algorithm, so that the effect of varying the number of data objects can be deduced without concern about the absolute time any particular execution will take.

Dealing with arbitrary constants is not useful for a relative measure of performance. In any comparison, they will cancel out. For instance, suppose it is known for some algorithm for which $n \geq 1$ that

$$T(n) = k_0 + k_1 n + k_2 n^2 .$$

Regardless of the relative sizes of k_0, k_1, and k_2, it will always be possible to find k_2' such that

$$T(n) \leq k_2' n^2 .$$

Also, with $n = 1$, the smallest meaningful value, it is clear that

$$T(n) \geq k_0 + k_1 + k_2 .$$

These expressions giving the time performance of the algorithm for the smallest value of n and for arbitrarily large n will be true regardless of the values of the constants. These asymptotic values of the complexity are the ones of interest. They have the benefit of elegance and simplicity. They capture the performance of the algorithm at the two extreme values that n can have.

Example:

Consider the following program part that finds the largest element in an array. The statements of the program are numbered so they can be conveniently referenced.

```
1    var A: array 1..n of int
2    var big: int

3    big := A(1)
4    for i: 2..n
5        if A(i) > big then
6            big := A(i)
7        end if
8    end for
```

Statements 1 and 2 take no time when the program executes because they are messages to the compiler about the nature of the data. They translate into no run-time instructions. Statement 3 is executed once. Statements 4, 5, 7, and 8 are executed each time the for loop is traversed. This happens for i equal to $2, 3, 4,$ $\ldots$, n, a total of $n - 1$ times.

The object of the exercise is to derive the execution time of the program as a function of n. The number of times Statement 6 is executed distinguishes between the best case, the worst case, and the average case.

Best Case

In the best case, Statement 6 is never executed, because A(1) is the largest element.

Worst Case

The worst case executes Statement 6 each time around the loop. This will happen only if the data in the array is sorted in increasing order, and if there are no duplicate elements in it.

Average Case

It is plausible to reason that in the average case, Statement 6 will be executed half the times the loop is traversed. The actual average will depend upon factors not necessarily known, such as the number of duplicate entries in the array. In the special case in which all the array elements are equal it will never be executed. For the purposes of this example, it will be assumed that there are no duplicates, and that the data is randomly ordered. Then Statement 6 will be executed about half the times around the loop.

Let the time taken to execute Statement j be τ_j. The execution time of the program part follows.

$$\text{best} \quad \tau_3 + (n-1)(\tau_4 + \tau_5 + \tau_7 + \tau_8)$$

$$\text{worst} \quad \tau_3 + (n-1)(\tau_4 + \tau_5 + \tau_6 + \tau_7 + \tau_8)$$

$$\text{average} \quad \tau_3 + (n-1)(\tau_4 + \tau_5 + \tau_7 + \tau_8) + \frac{(n-1)}{2}\tau_6$$

Each of these cases is of the form $k_0 + k_1 n$. Obviously, $n \geq 1$. Asymptotically, $k_0 + k_1 \leq T(n) \leq k_1' n$, where $k_1' = k_0 + k_1$.

2.2.1. Notation for Time Complexity

If $T(n)$ is the time it takes an algorithm to process n objects, then $T(n) = O(f(n))$ will mean that $T(n)$ is bounded above by the function $f(n)$. The notation $O(f(n))$ is pronounced as *order of f(n)*. Also, $T(n) = \Omega(g(n))$ will mean that $T(n)$ is bounded below by the function $g(n)$. The notation $\Omega(g(n))$ is pronounced as *omega of g(n)*. In these notes, $g(n)$ will not be considered further, because in practical situations the longest execution time of an algorithm is usually far more significant than the shortest.

The function $f(n)$ is the upper bound on the *time complexity* of the algorithm. The algorithm will take a time that is not longer than $\kappa \times f(n)$, for some constant κ. This upper bound on processing time as a function of n is obviously an important measure of the effectiveness of an algorithm, but it is not the whole story. Often it will be found that two algorithms are of the same time complexity, but one is much preferable to the other for secondary reasons. For instance, two sorting algorithms may be the same order, but one might re-arrange identical data objects, while the other might not. Alternatively, the constant κ could be much larger for one algorithm than for another. These issues could be important in some applications. The choice of the appropriate algorithm is a major factor in software engineering.

As n increases, the time complexity of the algorithm becomes extremely important. From the table below, it is evident that algorithms with exponential complexity can become useless for large n, because in practice they would take too long to execute.

n	$\log n$	$n \log n$	n^2	n^3	2^n	$n!$
1	0	0	1	1	2	1
4	2	8	16	64	16	24
16	4	64	256	4096	65536	2092×10^{10}
32	5	160	1024	32768	4295×10^6	6579×10^{32}
1024	10	10240	1048576	1074×10^6	1798×10^{305}	5418×10^{2636}

It is not uncommon to need to deal with thousands of data objects. An $O(n \log n)$ algorithm can take several decimal orders of magnitude less time to do this than an $O(n^2)$ algorithm would. On the other hand, this difference disappears if there are a few tens of data objects, given that the $O(n \log n)$ algorithm is certain to be more complicated than the $O(n^2)$ one.

Some problems, known as *hard* problems, are intrinsically exponential in nature. In practice, these problems often can only be solved in an approximate way. There exist problems with complexity worse than $O(2^n)$; for instance, problems with complexity $O(n!)$, $O(n^n)$, and $O(2^{2^n})$ are known. In practice, such problems must be simplified in order to be solved.

2.2.2. An Example Involving a Matrix

This section will present three ways to raise a quantity to a given integer power. The problem is an important one, but here it is used to provide a definite example of complexity and to develop a formal technique of analyzing algorithms.

In general, the quantity to be raised to a power could be anything for which the notion of raise to a power is meaningful, like a
number or a matrix. Raising a number to a power occurs frequently
in the analysis of physical phenomena, but it is perhaps not obvious
that a power of a matrix is also sometimes required.

The abstract machine shown below is a simplified version of one
that arose as part of an actual experiment. The experiment was performed to investigate the performance of a computer-to-computer
communications network. The abstract machine was developed as
part of the analysis of a particular hardware component that had
been constructed to generate data packets for the network. It has
been simplified to concentrate on fundamentals and to ignore the
finer points of the actual experiment that was performed.

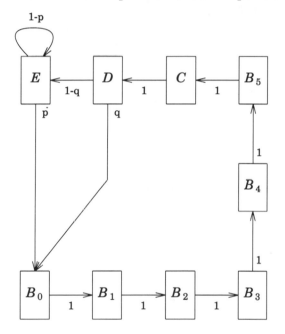

This kind of abstract machine is constructed from *states* and
transitions between states. Each state is shown as a box with the
state name printed inside. The states are named so they can be
referred to in a simple way. In machines like this, states represent a
particular situation or action that happens in a real piece of
hardware. In this sense, the machine shown above is an abstraction
of the actual hardware. This kind of abstract machine is called a
discrete Markov chain. What happens at any state is not affected by

anything that has happened previously or by the properties of any other state. The machine has no memory elements.

The machine is driven by a clock that forces movement from state to state. Each state in the machine is occupied for exactly one clock tick, and then a transition, shown by an arrow, moves the machine from its present state to its next state. Each transition has shown beside it the probability of taking that particular path. For instance, in state E, the next state will be either state B_0 with probability p, or a return to state E with probability $1-p$. Since the machine always moves to a new state at each clock tick, the probabilities associated with the transitions leaving each state always add to 1. In the example, the probabilities are given in symbolic form. These probabilities are the parameters of the experiment, and changing any of them will result in a new experiment.

State E corresponds to the hardware idling with probability $1-p$. However, with probability p a transition is made to state B_0. In reality, the value of p is equal to the probability of a particular random event happening in the hardware. The machine will move successively through states B_0, B_1, and so on, to state B_5 and eventually to state C. In each of the B states it will spend one clock tick, so the excursion from entering state B_0 to arriving at state C will take six clock ticks. The packets that this machine would generate would be six clock ticks long. The succession of six states B_0 through B_5 are all similar. They represent the generation of a data packet to be sent over the network. In the actual experiment, packets were hundreds of clock ticks long rather than 6 clock ticks long, and so there were many more members of the B states.

The arrival in state C corresponds to the end of the packet. States C and D model a two-tick pause that is required to happen at the end of a packet. From state D, the machine may force another packet to start immediately by returning to state B_0 with probability q, another parameter of the experiment. Alternatively, it may enter state E with probability $1-q$, and idle there waiting for another occurrence of the event that signals the proper time to start a packet.

The behaviour of machines like this can be summarized in a matrix called the next-state matrix. Both the rows and the columns of the next-state matrix are indexed with the set of all states in the machine. The row index is the current state, and the column index is the next state. An entry in the matrix is the probability of the row-indexed state being immediately succeeded by the column-indexed state. The next-state matrix for the example is shown in Table 2.1.

| Table 2.1: Next-state Matrix for the Example. | | | | | | | | |
	B_0	B_1	B_2	B_3	B_4	B_5	C	D	E
B_0	0	1	0	0	0	0	0	0	0
B_1	0	0	1	0	0	0	0	0	0
B_2	0	0	0	1	0	0	0	0	0
B_3	0	0	0	0	1	0	0	0	0
B_4	0	0	0	0	0	1	0	0	0
B_5	0	0	0	0	0	0	1	0	0
C	0	0	0	0	0	0	0	1	0
D	q	0	0	0	0	0	0	0	$1-q$
E	p	0	0	0	0	0	0	0	$1-p$

If π_s is the probability of finding the machine in any state

$$s \in \{ B_0, B_1, B_2, B_3, B_4, B_5, C, D, E \}$$

the nine linearly dependent equations shown in Table 2.2 that relate the probabilities can be found easily by examining the next-state matrix.

Table 2.2: The Linearly Dependent Equations for the Example.		
$\pi_{B_0} = p\,\pi_E + q\,\pi_D$	$\pi_{B_3} = \pi_{B_2}$	$\pi_C = \pi_{B_5}$
$\pi_{B_1} = \pi_{B_0}$	$\pi_{B_4} = \pi_{B_3}$	$\pi_D = \pi_C$
$\pi_{B_2} = \pi_{B_1}$	$\pi_{B_5} = \pi_{B_4}$	$\pi_E = (1-q)\,\pi_D + (1-p)\,\pi_E$

Also, the machine must always be in some state, so

$$\pi_{B_0} + \pi_{B_1} + \pi_{B_2} + \pi_{B_3} + \pi_{B_4} + \pi_{B_5} + \pi_C + \pi_D + \pi_E = 1$$

The solution of this final equation and any eight of the first nine linearly dependent equations gives the probability of finding the machine in each state if it is allowed to run freely. Suppose this is done and the results are stored in a nine-element vector Π. The elements of Π will be

$$\pi_{B_0} = \pi_{B_1} = \pi_{B_2} = \pi_{B_3} = \pi_{B_4} = \pi_{B_5} = \pi_C = \pi_D = \frac{p}{8p + (1-q)}$$

$$\pi_E = \frac{1-q}{8p + (1-q)}$$

Call the next-state matrix M. Suppose time is measured in clock ticks from some instant called the epoch. At the epoch the probability the machine is in each state is known and stored in Π. The future behaviour of the machine after the epoch can be predicted as shown in Table 2.3. The second column shows how to find a vector Σ giving the probability of being in each of the states at the given time after the epoch.

In the actual calculations that were done for the experiment, the matrix and the power that the matrix was raised to were much larger. It is apparent that an efficient method of raising the matrix to a large power is required. The methods that follow show three programs to do this. Each program uses a different basic technique and consequently have they have different performance characteristics.

2.3. RAISE-TO-POWER DEFINITIONS

Let a be some quantity that can be multiplied by things of similar type. Define $a^0 \equiv 1$. Let $a^1 = a \times a^0$, $a^2 = a \times a^1$, and in general for any $j > 0$, $a^j = a \times a^{j-1}$. a^j is said to be a raised to the jth power. j is called the *exponent* and a is called the *base.*. This definition can easily be extended to cases when the exponent is negative if there is some quantity b such that $b \times a = 1$, so that $a^j = b^{-j}$.

Table 2.3: State Probabilities after the Epoch.	
Time after the Epoch (clock ticks)	Probability Vector Σ
0	Π
1	$\Pi \times M$
2	$\Pi \times M^2$
3	$\Pi \times M^3$
4	$\Pi \times M^4$
...	...
k	$\Pi \times M^k$

The case when $a = 0$ is an example of a difficult situation. By the definition above, $0^0 \equiv 1$, while for $j > 0$, $0^j = 0$. When $j < 0$, 0^j is undefined because of the difficulty of division by zero.

The three ways to raise to a power will be presented so that the type of the base is a detail that can be dealt with when an actual program is written. Consequently, it is assumed that somewhere in the program *basetype* is declared. Also, it is assumed there is a

```
function basemult(a,b: basetype):basetype
```

that accepts two arguments of type basetype and returns their product, also of type basetype. It will be assumed that basemult takes a constant time to do its job for any particular instance of a basetype. For the purpose of these overviews of the algorithms, the details of the basetype and of basemult are of no concern. In a real program where basetype and basemult are known, actual facts about them may alter the algorithm in small detail.

For simplicity, it will be assumed that the exponent is known to be non-negative. If this assumption is not made we would need to know a great deal more about basetype.

2.4. BRUTE FORCE — firstRaise

The first algorithm is a direct application of the definition. It is known that $a^j = a \times a^{j-1}$. This can be used repetitively to calculate a^j.

```
% Raise a quantity of type basetype to a non-negative power.
  function firstRaise(a: basetype, j: int)

          var i: int     % i is an internal version of j
          var ans: basetype     % the result is developed here
1         i := j - 1
2         ans := 1.0       % 1.0 means the value of a⁰

3         loop
4             exit when i < 0

              % multiply by yet another a
5             ans := basemult(ans, a)

              % count to see if enough multiplies have been done
6             i -= 1
7         end loop

8         result ans

  end firstRaise
```

It is not hard to see that this program will call basemult j times, because it traverses the `loop` j times. If j is a small integer, say 2 or 5, the time spent looping the `loop` would not be a problem. But if j =1024, this program will traverse the loop 1024 times, each traverse taking a constant time.

The program firstRaise will always do j loops of the `loop`. The rest of the program will take a constant time, independent of j. As a consequence of these things, two constants k_1 and k_2 exist such that $T_{\text{firstRaise}}(j) = k_1 + k_2 \times j$. The most important thing about this equation is its behaviour as a function of j. The program firstRaise is said to have a complexity that is linear in j. This property of firstRaise is written

$$T_{\text{firstRaise}}(j) = O(j).$$

Formally the notation $T = O(j)$ means that there exists some constant κ such that $T \leq \kappa \times j$. Such a constant can evidently be found for the case for $T_{\text{firstRaise}}(j)$.

2.5. USING RECURSION — secondRaise
Among the consequences of the raise to power definition is that if j is an even integer, then $a^{2j} = a^j \times a^j$, and if j is an odd integer, then $a^{2j+1} = a^j \times a^j \times a$. These two facts, and the programming technique of recursion, can be used to produce a more efficient algorithm.

```
    % Raise a quantity of type basetype to a non-negative power.
      function secondRaise(a: basetype, j: int)

          var temp: basetype      % a temporary

          % the answer is obvious if j=0 or j=1
1         if j <= 1 then
2             if j = 1 then
3                 result a
4             else
5                 result 1
6             end if
7         end if

8         temp := secondRaise(a, j div 2)

9         if j mod 2 = 0 then
10            result basemult(temp,temp)
11        else
12            result basemult( basemult(temp,temp), a)
13        end if

      end secondRaise
```

It is necessary to examine the algorithm in detail to find the complexity of secondRaise. The first step is to decide what costly activities the algorithm does. The test to see if $j \leq 1$ is quick, and since j is usually large, it will result in bypassing the rest of the if statement. The recursive call of secondRaise could take a long time. The operation basemult is called once if j is even and twice if j is odd. The complexity of basemult is unknown; it depends on the complexity of multiplying two quantities of type basetype together. Thus, the two things that are of most concern are how many times secondRaise is called and how many times basemult is called.

Table 2.4 shows three cases with basetype a real number, listing the successive calls to secondRaise and to basemult. In each case, the real number 1.05 is being raised to the indicated power. The calls to secondRaise are given explicitly, while the calls to basemult are shown using the more conventional × symbol.

Table 2.4: Trace of secondRaise.			
Step	$j=63$	$j=64$	$j=65$
0	secondRaise(1.05,63)	secondRaise(1.05,64)	secondRaise(1.05,65)
1	secondRaise(1.05,31)	secondRaise(1.05,32)	secondRaise(1.05,32)
2	secondRaise(1.05,15)	secondRaise(1.05,16)	secondRaise(1.05,16)
3	secondRaise(1.05,7)	secondRaise(1.05,8)	secondRaise(1.05,8)
4	secondRaise(1.05,3)	secondRaise(1.05,4)	secondRaise(1.05,4)
5	secondRaise(1.05,1)	secondRaise(1.05,2)	secondRaise(1.05,2)
6	(1.05×1.05)×1.05	secondRaise(1.05,1)	secondRaise(1.05,1)
7	(1.1576×1.1576)×1.05	1.05×1.05	1.05×1.05
8	(1.4071×1.4071)×1.05	1.1025×1.1025	1.1025×1.1025
9	(2.0789×2.0789)×1.05	1.2155×1.2155	1.2155×1.2155
10	(4.5380×4.5380)×1.05	1.4775×1.4775	1.4775×1.4775
11	21.6235	2.1829×2.1829	2.1829×2.1829
12		4.7649×4.7649	(4.7649×4.7649)×1.05
13		22.7046	23.8399
second-Raise calls	6	7	7
base-mult calls	10	6	7

The number of secondRaise calls can be predicted easily. The recursive call to secondRaise halves the value of the exponent it uses as an argument. There will be an integer κ such that the original value of the exponent, j in the program, satisfies the inequality

$$2^{\kappa-1} \le j < 2^{\kappa} \ .$$

All terms in this equality can be repeatedly divided by 2, ending up after k such divisions with

$$\frac{2^{\kappa-1}}{2^k} \le \frac{j}{2^k} < \frac{2^{\kappa}}{2^k} \ .$$

This can be simplified to give

$$2^{\kappa-1-k} \le \frac{j}{2^k} < 2^{\kappa-k} \ .$$

If k is chosen such that $\kappa-k = 1$, then

$$1 = 2^0 \le \frac{j}{2^k} < 2^1 = 2 \ .$$

Thus, $k = \kappa-1$ divisions by 2 will bring the second argument in the recursive call, which is the exponent, to the integer 1. The original call to secondRaise is not included in this count, so overall secondRaise is called κ times. For $j = 63$, $\kappa = 6$. For $j = 64$ and $j = 65$, $\kappa = 7$. In analytical form, $\kappa = 1+\text{floor}(\log_2 j)$. The count shown in the table agrees with the results of this equation. As an example of this, $\log_2 63 = 5.97728$, so $1+\text{floor}(5.97728) = 1+5 = 6$.

The number of calls to basemult is a little more difficult. It is easy to see that each time that secondRaise is called, except the last, there will be one or two calls to basemult. The exponent is halved $\kappa-1$ times. If the exponent for a call to secondRaise is even, there will be one call of basemult. If the exponent for a call to secondRaise is odd, basemult will be called twice.

Worst Case

In the worst case, every time the exponent is halved an odd number will result. There will be a total of $2(\kappa-1)$ calls to basemult. This situation happens when $j = 2^{\kappa}-1$, as when $j = 63 = 2^6-1$, $\kappa = 6$, and there were $2 \times 5 = 10$ calls to basemult.

Best Case

In the best case, every time the exponent is originally halved an even number will result. There will be one call to basemult for each of the first $\kappa-1$ calls to secondRaise, which means $\kappa-1$ calls to basemult. This situation happens when $j = 2^{\kappa-1}$, as when $j = 64 = 2^6$, $\kappa = 7$, and there were 6 calls to basemult.

Average Case

It is assumed that all exponents are equally probable. For any particular value of κ, all the values of j satisfying the inequality $2^{\kappa-1} \le j < 2^{\kappa}$ are equally probable. There are $2^{\kappa-1}$ values that j can have in this range. If we use 1 to indicate a single call to basemult, and 2 to imply that two calls to basemult are made, a sequence of $\kappa-1$ 1's and 2's will correspond to a unique j in the range. For instance, for $\kappa = 7$, the sequence 1,1,1,1,1,2 corresponds to $j = 65$. There are $2^{\kappa-1}$ such sequences of $\kappa-1$ 1's and 2's. From this, it may be concluded that it is equally probable that there will be one call to basemult or two calls to basemult at any call to secondRaise. Thus, on average there will be 1.5 calls to basemult for each call to secondRaise except the last. This means that on average there will be $1.5(\kappa-1)$ calls to basemult.

The complexity of secondRaise is, on average, the sum of the costs of the number of calls to secondRaise and the number of calls to basemult.

$$T_{secondRaise}(j) = k_1 + k_2\,\kappa + 1.5\,k_3\,(\kappa-1)$$

$$= k_4 + k_5\,\kappa$$

$$= k_6 + k_7\,(1+\text{floor}\,(\log_2 j\,)$$

$$= k_8 + k_9\,\text{floor}\,(\log_2 j\,)$$

$$= O(\text{floor}\,(\log_2 j\,))$$

$$= O(\log_2 j)$$

This complexity also applies to the best and worst cases.

Because it is logarithmic in complexity, secondRaise is a lot better than firstRaise. If $j = 1024$, secondRaise has a complexity proportional to 10, over 100 times better than firstRaise.

2.6. FINESSING THE EXPONENT — thirdRaise

The only problem with secondRaise is the recursive calls to itself that are required. The program thirdRaise is quicker than secondRaise because it need not be recursive, and so can avoid the overhead cost associated with numerous procedure calls.

The idea behind thirdRaise is to convert the exponent to a number in base-2 notation. The 1-digits in this base-2 number will indicate which powers of the base must be multiplied together to

```
     % Raise a quantity of type basetype to a non-negative power.
     function thirdRaise(a: basetype, j: int)

          var pow: basetype     % the base-2 powers of a
          var ans: basetype     % the answer
          var i: int     % a work integer

1         i := j
2         ans := 1          % a raised to the zero
3         pow := a     % a raised to the 2**0

4         loop

              % Exit when the exponent is zero
5             exit when i = 0

              % What is the lowest remaining base-2 digit?
6             if i mod 2 = 1 then

7                 if ans not = 1 then
                      % If ans is not 1 then need to basemult
8                     ans := basemult(ans, pow)
9                 else
                      % If ans is 1 then don't need to basemult
10                    ans := pow

11                end if

12            end if

              % exit when i=1.  This is the normal exit.
13            exit when i = 1

              % square the pow
14            pow := basemult(pow, pow)

              % Halve i
15            i := i div 2

16        end loop

17   result ans

     end thirdRaise
```

Figure 2.1: The thirdRaise Program.

develop the result. As an example, suppose 1.05^{71} is to be computed. The exponent is

$$71_{10} = 1000111_2 = 1\times2^6 + 0\times2^5 + 0\times2^4 + 0\times2^3 + 1\times2^2 + 1\times2^1 + 1\times2^0 \ .$$

Thus,

$$1.05^{71} = 1.05^{64} \times 1.05^4 \times 1.05^2 \times 1.05^1 \ .$$

The powers of the base can be built up continually and multiplied together as needed. The thirdRaise program is shown in Figure 2.1.

The potentially costly operations in thirdRaise are the mod function in the if predicate in the loop, the call to basemult in the then clause of the if, the call to basemult at the end of the loop, and the div function at the end of the loop.

The first of these is done each time the loop body is started. The third and fourth of these are done each time around the loop. A count of the number of times the loop is looped will give their contribution to the complexity. The second costly operation, the call to basemult in the then clause of the if, is done at best never ($j = 0$), at worst each time around the loop ($j = 2^\kappa-1$), and on average half the times around the loop. Following the same line of reasoning that was used in the analysis of secondRaise, it is not difficult to show that the loop is started κ times.

Hence, with the understanding that the constants will differ for the worst, best, and average cases,

$$T_{\text{thirdRaise}}(j) = k_1 + k_2\times\kappa$$

$$= O(\log_2 j) \ ,$$

exactly the same complexity as secondRaise. The accompanying table, similar to the one shown in the analysis of secondRaise, shows the calculation of the same results as those done for secondRaise. The table shows only the calls to basemult because these are most likely to be significantly more costly than the mod and div operations, unless basetype is a simple number.

For thirdRaise, the number of basemult calls is the same in each case as the number needed by secondRaise. However, it is clear that thirdRaise would be considerably faster than secondRaise. Both secondRaise and thirdRaise are $O(\log_2 j)$, but secondRaise requires $\kappa-1$ recursive calls of itself. Normally, procedure calls and function calls are quite expensive, and thirdRaise is not recursive. The algorithm thirdRaise is better for all exponents and for any basetype. A quick or slow basemult will affect both algorithms equally.

Table 2.5: Trace of thirdRaise.			
Step	$j=63$	$j=64$	$j=65$
0	ans = 1 pow = 1.05	ans = 1 pow = 1.05	ans = 1 pow = 1.05
1	ans = 1.05 pow = 1.05×1.05 = 1.1025	pow = 1.1025	ans = 1.05 pow = 1.1025
2	ans = 1.05×1.1025 = 1.1576 pow = 1.1025×1.1025 = 1.2155	pow = 1.2155	pow = 1.2155
3	ans = 1.1576×1.2155 = 1.4071 pow = 1.2155×1.2155 = 1.4775	pow = 1.4775	pow = 1.4775
4	ans = 1.4071×1.4775 = 2.0789 pow = 1.4775×1.4775 = 2.1829	pow = 2.1829	pow = 2.1829
5	ans = 2.0789×2.1829 = 4.5380 pow = 2.1829×2.1829 = 4.7649	pow = 4.7649	pow = 4.7649
6	ans = 4.5380×4.7649 = 21.6235	pow = 22.7046	pow = 22.7046
7		ans = 22.7046	ans = 23.8399
base-mult calls	10	6	7

2.7. A REPRISE ON THE RAISES

Very often the use of a little thought can make an astonishing improvement in efficiency. In the brute-force firstRaise no attempt was made to be efficient. Efficiency improved with both secondRaise and thirdRaise. Undoubtedly the most significant thing that has been demonstrated with the Raises is the benefit that can be realized from the analysis of an algorithm. It is an important lesson, and should be well learned.

SecondRaise uses a method called *divide and conquer* that will be studied again later. Generally, as will be seen, divide and conquer will result in an improvement in efficiency similar to the one seen with secondRaise. It is frequently used because of this feature.

ThirdRaise uses a peculiarity of the problem to re-cast it in another notation. This allows the algorithm to exploit a feature of the new notation that improved its efficiency. The method is generally called *algebraic simplification*. It is rarely applicable, because most problems cannot be simplified as effectively as this one can. Nevertheless, with serendipity, it can be very effective, as is seen with thirdRaise.

The example of the abstract machine was used to introduce the raise-to-power problem. It would clearly run most quickly if thirdRaise were used. In many cases, secondRaise would be not much worse, because the time to do a basemult will often dominate all other operations. In these cases, the use of firstRaise will result in a disastrously slow program.

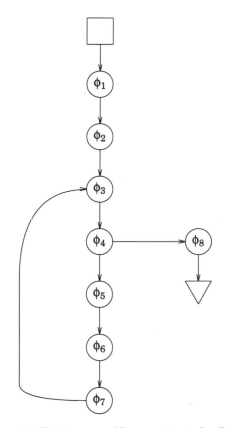

Figure 2.2: The Progress of Computation in firstRaise.

2.8. KIRCHOFF'S LAW AND INVARIANTS

In the case of complicated programs it is not always evident how many times any statement is executed. Fortunately, there exists a method of analysis that will help develop this information. In simple cases, an added bonus is that a variation on the method can be used to verify that the program is correct, in the sense that what is calculated in the loops in the program is what is intended. The method is best explained by example, and both firstRaise and thirdRaise will be used as illustrations.

2.8.1. Analysis of firstRaise

For programs that are as short and as simple as firstRaise the method of analysis is rather more pedantic than is strictly necessary. Nevertheless, it is instructive to follow it as an introduction to the method.

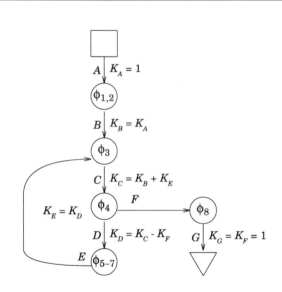

Figure 2.3: The Progress of Computation in firstRaise, Simplified by Combining Sequential Non-Branching Steps.

2.8.1.1. *Complexity of firstRaise*

In the program listing of firstRaise, each executable statement is numbered. The progress of the computation can be represented as in Figure 2.2. Each circle in the figure represents one of the statements in the program. The cost of executing a statement is usually measured in time, although other measures like space are sometimes important. A variable ϕ_i giving the cost of each statement is associated with every circle. These variables are shown in the figure. The structure of the figure represents the flow of control through the program as it is executed. Possible paths of execution are shown by arrows from one statement to those that can follow it.

Sequences of several statements that, once entered, must be executed sequentially, like Statement 1 and Statement 2, can be combined by adding their execution times. If this is done for Figure 2.2, the simplified result shown in Figure 2.3 is obtained. The circles in Figure 2.3 now represent groups of statements. To imply this they will be called *blocks* rather than statements.

In Figure 2.3, the paths between blocks have been identified with a letter. Let K_i represent the number of times that the path i is traversed in an execution of the program. Given values for the K's and for the ϕ's, it is possible to deduce the running time of the program as

$$T_{\text{program}} = \sum_m \left[\phi_m \times \sum_{\text{paths}} K_{\text{paths entering } m} \right] .$$

Table 2.6: Conservation Equations.	
$K_A = 1$	$K_E = K_D$
$K_B = K_A$	$K_G = K_F$
$K_C = K_B + K_E$	$1 = K_G$
$K_D + K_F = K_C$	

The critical step of the analysis is now at hand. For any block in the figure, the number of times the block is left must exactly equal the number of times it is entered. This is a situation that should be reminiscent of Kirchoff's law in the analysis of electric circuits. Such laws are called *laws of conservation*. They occur frequently in physical models that represent the flow of some real or abstract substance. Each time the flow of control in a program enters a block it must also leave the block. Using this law of conservation, it is easy to write the equations shown in Table 2.6. These seven equations in seven unknowns are not independent. By simple algebraic manipulation, it is easy to show that $K_C = 1 + K_D$. In a figure like that shown above, a path that closes on itself is called a *cycle*. The only cycle in the above figure is that following paths C, D, and E. This cycle obviously corresponds to the loop in the program. It is possible to show that there will be one equation remaining to be solved for each cycle in the program. An analysis must now be done to determine how many times such cycles are traversed.

The algebra that developed the previous equation also shows that $K_A = 1$, $K_B = 1$, $K_E = K_D$, $K_F = 1$, and $K_G = 1$. This is the limit of the help Kirchoff's equations provide. To get the final result, a value for K_C or for K_D is needed. Examining the program, it is clear that the test in Statement 4 will provide that information. K_C and K_D are related to the number of times the loop body is entered. The loop is as follows:

```
loop
    exit when i < 0

    % multiply by yet another a
    ans := basemult(ans, a)

    % count to see if enough multiplies have been done
    i -= 1
end loop
```

When the loop is being executed, the imaginary point in the body of the loop that is first executed, and that is returned to for each time around the loop, is called the *head* of the loop. At the head of the loop, it is always true that a k can be found such that $i = (j-1) - k$. This is certainly true for $k = 0$, because initially $i = j-1$. Examination of the loop shows that it is true for $k = 1, 2, 3, \cdots$.

It is known from the statements in the loop that i decreases by 1 in each successive pass and that the loop finishes the first time $i < 0$. The first time when $i < 0$ is when $i = -1$, and this is when the loop ends. Substituting $i = -1$ into $i = (j-1) - k$ gives $k = j$ as the value of k to be associated with the last time the loop is entered. Thus the head of the loop is entered with k successively equal $0, 1, 2, 3, \cdots, j$, for a total of $j+1$ times. From this, it is concluded that $K_C = j+1$, because K_C is the number of times the head of the loop is entered. Consequently, $K_A = 1$, $K_B = 1$, $K_C = j+1$, $K_D = j$, $K_E = j$, $K_F = 1$, and $K_G = 1$.

Each block in the program is executed each time it is entered, so the running time of the program is

$$T_{\text{firstRaise}}(j) = K_A\,\phi_{1,2} + (K_B + K_E)\,\phi_3 + K_C\,\phi_4 + K_D\,\phi_{5,6,7} + K_F\,\psi_8$$

$$= \phi_{1,2} + (1+j)\,\phi_3 + (1+j)\,\phi_4 + j\,\phi_{5,6,7} + \phi_8$$

$$= (\phi_{1,2} + \phi_3 + \phi_4 + \phi_8) + (\phi_3 + \phi_4 + \phi_{5,6,7})\,j$$

$$= O(j)\ .$$

This result agrees with that found by the less formal method. Often, the formal method is useful to show exactly which statements in the program are consuming time. It is especially valuable if a comparison is being done to determine the complexity of the program for several environments. For instance, if a hardware enhancement to speed up multiplication is being considered, the effect of this change on a program could be quite accurately predicted.

2.8.1.2. Loop Invariant in firstRaise

There is more information that can be deduced from the analysis of the previous section. It is possible to find an expression that always has the same value at the head of loop. Such an expression is called a *loop invariant*.

It was seen above that at the head of the loop, it is always true that a k can be found such that $i = (j-1)-k$. It is also true that at the head of the loop $\text{ans} = a^k$. These equations are certainly true for $k = 0$, because initially $i = j-1$ and $\text{ans} = 1 = a^0$. Examination of the loop shows that they are also true for $k = 1,2,3, \cdots$.

Eliminating k from $i = (j-1)-k$ and $\text{ans} = a^k$ gives the loop invariant as $[\ \log_a \text{ans} = (j-1)-i\ ] = \text{true}$. The loop ends when $i = -1$ and $k = j$. At the end of the loop, $j = \log_a \text{ans}$ so $a^j = \text{ans}$. The program has been shown to be "correct" to the extent that the analysis can show that desirable feature.

The purpose of identifying the loop invariant is to make sure that the proper expressions are used to find out what the loop computes. In loops that have an index variable that progressively changes with each traversal of the loop, like i in firstRaise, it is usually possible to follow the technique used above and relate the value of the index variable to whatever else the loop computes. The identification of the loop invariant serves to ensure that the reasoning that is involved has been done properly.

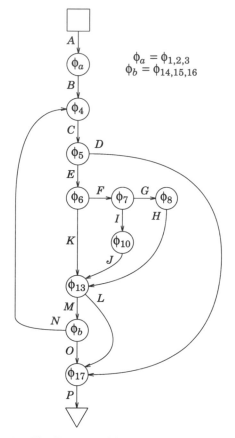

$$\phi_a = \phi_{1,2,3}$$
$$\phi_b = \phi_{14,15,16}$$

Figure 2.4: The Progress of Computation in thirdRaise.

2.8.2. Analysis of thirdRaise

As a second example, the analysis of thirdRaise proceeds as shown in Figure 2.4. In the program listing of thirdRaise, each executable statement is numbered. The progress of the computation can be represented by the accompanying diagram, in which ϕ_a represents $\phi_{1,2,3}$ and ϕ_b represents $\phi_{14,15,16}$.

   This figure is much more complicated than that representing firstRaise. The analysis is correspondingly complicated. As in the analysis of firstRaise, $K_A = K_P = 1$. Also, because of the way the program is arranged, the exit from the loop will always be due to one of the exit statements. At Statement 5, an exit from the loop occurs if $i = 0$. At Statement 13, an exit from the loop occurs if $i = 1$. No other tests can result in an exit, and so $K_O = 0$. The 12 conservation equations are shown in Table 2.7. These equations are easily simplified as shown in equations 13 through 18.

$$K_C = 1 + K_M \tag{13}$$

$$K_D + K_E = K_C \tag{14}$$

$$K_F + K_K = K_E \tag{15}$$

$$K_G + K_I = K_F \tag{16}$$

$$K_L + K_M = K_K + K_I + K_G \tag{17}$$

$$1 = K_D + K_L \tag{18}$$

   Equation 13 is concerned with the number of times the head of the loop is re-entered from the end of the loop. The loop starts with $i = j$, and each circuit of the loop contains Statement 15. It is not hard to reason that for $j > 0$ the number of times path K_N is taken is $floor(\log_2 j)$. K_N is equal to K_M which is now known, so K_C is also known.

   Equation 14 is concerned with Statement 5, in which a test is made to short-circuit the rest of the loop for the special case $i = 0$.

Table 2.7: Conservation Equations for thirdRaise.			
1	$K_A = 1$	7	$K_H = K_G$
2	$K_B = K_A$	8	$K_J = K_I$
3	$K_C = K_B + K_N$	9	$K_L + K_M = K_K + K_J + K_H$
4	$K_D + K_E = K_C$	10	$K_O = 0$
5	$K_F + K_K = K_E$	11	$K_P = K_D + K_L + K_O$
6	$K_G + K_I = K_F$	12	$1 = K_P$

This case is not of particular concern, because it will not arise often. Let $j > 0$ so that the special case does not exist for the purposes of this analysis. If this is done, $K_D = 0$ and $K_C = K_E$.

Equation 15 corresponds to Statement 6. For the average case, i will be odd or even an equal number of times, so $K_F = K_K = 0.5 K_E$.

The first time it is evaluated the predicate in Statement 7 will be false. Statement 10 will be executed exactly once, and all further evaluations of the predicate of Statement 7 will be true. When the predicate is true, Statement 8 will be executed. This means that $K_I = K_J = 1$, with equation 16 becoming $K_I + 1 = K_F$.

It is apparent that an exit from the loop is taken only once. If the exit is not from Statement 5, which has been ruled out because of the special nature of $j = 0$, it must be via Statement 13. This means $K_L = 1$. K_M is known from the above discussion of equation 13, so if all the K's that are known so far are combined, equation 17 becomes $1 + \text{floor}(\log_2 j) = 0.5 K_E + 1 + (0.5 K_E - 1)$. This solves all unknowns, and the K's are as follows:

$$K_A = 1$$

$$K_B = 1$$

$$K_C = 1 + \text{floor}(\log_2 j)$$

$$K_D = 0$$

$$K_E = 1 + \text{floor}(\log_2 j)$$

$$K_F = 0.5(1 + \text{floor}(\log_2 j))$$

$$K_G = 0.5(1 + \text{floor}(\log_2 j)) - 1$$

$$K_H = 0.5(1 + \text{floor}(\log_2 j)) - 1$$

$$K_I = 1$$

$$K_J = 1$$

$$K_K = 0.5(1 + \text{floor}(\log_2 j))$$

$$K_L = 1$$

$$K_M = \text{floor}(\log_2 j)$$

$$K_N = \text{floor}(\log_2 j)$$

$$K_O = 0$$

$$K_P = 1 \quad .$$

If these values are summed as required, the result will be

$$T_{\text{thirdRaise}}(j) = O(\log_2 j).$$

This is the same result as was obtained informally.

The above solution is for the average case. The difference between the average, best, and worst cases is embodied in the analysis of Equation 15. When thirdRaise runs in its best case it will always take path K and never take path F. Conversely, running in the worst case it will always take path F and never take path K. All cases differ from each other by the value of a multiplicative constant, so all are $O(\log_2 j)$.

The loop invariants are not quite as simple to find as in firstRaise and will be left as an exercise.

2.9. WHICH RAISE IS BEST?
After reading the foregoing, it would seem sensible to conclude that thirdRaise is the best that can be done. This is not so! It has been seen that when $j = 63$, thirdRaise needs 10 calls to basemult. But

$$a^{63} = a^9 \times a^{18} \times a^{36}$$

$$= a^{3+3+3} \times a^{9+9} \times a^{18+18}.$$

$$= a^3 \times a^3 \times a^3 \times a^9 \times a^9 \times a^{18} \times a^{18}.$$

Thus, a^{63} can be computed by calculating
  (1) a^3, which takes two basemults, and
  (2) $a^9 = a^{3+3+3} = a^3 \times a^3 \times a^3$, which also takes two basemults, and
  (3) $a^{18} = a^9 \times a^9$, which takes one more basemult, and
  (4) $a^{36} = a^{18} \times a^{18}$, which takes yet another basemult, and
  (5) $a^{63} = a^9 \times a^{18} \times a^{36}$, which takes a final two basemults.
By this method, the number of basemults is eight, a saving of two.

It is interesting to try to find the minimum cost way to raise to a power. If a^j is desired, clearly the exponent can be split up into the sum of a sequence of integers that add to j. The split can be done in many ways, most of which would be poor if used in a raise to power calculation. For instance, $63 = 1+2+4+11+13+15+17$, not a big help. Every sequence worth considering will start with 1, representing the fact that a^1 is one of the arguments of the function, and consequently costs nothing to calculate. The two ways that a^{63} was calculated correspond to the sequences shown below.

(1)   1, 2, 4, 8, 16, 32. When the calculation was done, a^1 was mul-
       tiplied in turn by a^2, a^4, a^8, a^{16}, and a^{32}.

(2)   1, 2, 3, 6, 9, 18, 36. To calculate a^{63}, a^9 is multiplied by a^{18}
       and by a^{36}.

In the first case every power of a that is calculated multiplies the
answer developed so far. This is not always the situation, as seen in
the second case. It is not hard to see, in fact, that only if j is of the
form $2^k - 1$ for some k, does every power of a that is calculated multiply the answer that has been developed so far.

The minimum cost way to raise a to a power depends upon
finding a sequence of integers, say $j_0, j_1, \cdots, j_m$. The exponent will
be represented by the sum of some of the elements in the sequence.
This sequence can be assumed to be in ascending order, such that
$j_i < j_k$ if $i < k$. The sequence must meet the following criteria:

(1) $j_0 = 1$. This is an obvious requirement, because all of the cal-
       culations must ultimately depend on powers of a.

(2)   A selection of integers from the sequence must add to the
       desired exponent, $\displaystyle\sum_{\text{integers used}} j_i = j$.

(3)   For $i > 1$, $j_i = j_k + j_l$, where $k < i$ and $l < i$. Other than the first
       integer, 1, the integers are the sum of two of the previous
       integers. This must mean that $j_2 = 2$. It is allowable for k to
       equal l.

(4)   Let the members of the sequence that do not multiply the
       answer developed so far cost one multiply-unit (that's how
       many basemults it takes to calculate them). The members of
       the sequence that do multiply the answer developed so far cost
       the number of basemults it takes to calculate them (one), plus
       one multiply-unit because they multiply the answer. The first
       member of the sequence, 1, costs nothing. The element that
       initializes the answer does not incur a cost of one for multiply-
       ing the answer. The sum of all the cost units for the sequence
       must be minimized.

The two sequences that were given above to calculate a^{63} are
repeated below showing the cost units for each member as a subscript.

(1) 1_0 , 2_2 , 4_2 , 8_2 , 16_2 , 32_2 . The answer is initialized with a^1
       and every power developed multiplies the answer once. Each
       member except the first scores two cost units, one to calculate
       it and one to multiply the answer by it, for a total of ten.

(2) 1_0 , 2_1 , 3_1 , 6_1 , 9_1 , 18_2 , 36_2. The answer is initialized with
       a^9 and multiplied by a^{18} and by a^{36}. a^9 costs only one unit
       because it initializes the answer, but does not multiply it.

There are a total of eight cost units, even though there are more members in this sequence than in the previous one.

An effective way to compute the minimum cost sequence is not known, even though mathematicians have been working on the problem for many years. There are some special cases that are known. In practice, unless basemult is extremely expensive, it probably is not worth the effort to look for the minimum cost sequence. The one used in thirdRaise is good enough.

2.10. EXERCISES

1. Three arrays are declared by the statement

   ```
   var A,B,C: array 1..n,1..n of real
   ```

   Array C is the product of Arrays A and B if $C_{ij} = \sum_{k=1}^{n} A_{ik} \times B_{kj}$.
   Write a program to compute Array C. Find the complexity of this program. Let $n = 10^m$ for m a positive integer. If arithmetic operations on real numbers all take 1 microsecond, and all other operations take a negligible time, compare the time to find the product if $m = 1$ with the time to find the product if $m = 2$ and $m = 3$.

2. An insertion sort is a method of sorting data in an array A that works as follows. The array is conceptually divided into two subarrays $A_{1..j}$ and $A_{j+1..n}$. The first subarray $A_{1..j}$ is in sorted order. The second subarray $A_{j+1..n}$ remains to be sorted. When $j=1$ these conditions hold, because the first subarray has only one member.

sorted	not yet sorted

1   j $j+1$ n

Starting with $j=1$, A_{j+1} from the second subarray is inserted into the correct place in the first subarray, and j is increased by 1 until the entire second subarray has been inserted in the proper place in the first subarray.

If a linear search is used to find the correct place to insert in the first subarray, find the best case and the worst case complexity of insertion sort. If a binary search is used to find the correct place to insert in the first subarray, find the best case and the worst case complexity of insertion sort. For various values of n, which is the preferable method?

3. Two arrays are declared by the statement

    ```
    var A,B: array 1..n of int
    ```

    The data in each array is sorted such that $A_i \leq A_{i+1}$ and $B_i \leq B_{i+1}$. The arrays hold $2n$ elements in total. The median element is defined as the element that meets the requirement that $n-1$ of the elements are not greater than it, and n of the elements are not less than it.

    (a) Write a program that finds the median element by merging the two arrays. Find the complexity of this program.

    (b) Write a program that finds the median element without merging the two arrays. This may be done by writing a recursive program that compares the middle element of the two arrays, rejects half of each of them as candidates to contain the median, and calls itself with the other halves as arguments. Find the complexity of this program.

    (c) Compare the two programs that have been written. Which runs more quickly? Which occupies the least space? Which is better if n is small, and which is better if n is large?

4. In Section 2.8 the subject of better sequences of integers to add to the exponent was discussed. Show why the case of two successive integers in the sequence being equal to each other need not be considered.

5. Two elevators serve a building of three floors, called Floors 1, 2, and 3. The elevators operate without any call buttons, moving up and down according to some rules that are built in by the manufacturer. Each elevator can be at any floor with its doors open or with its doors closed. The motion of the elevators is governed by a clock. At any clock tick an elevator will do one of the following things:

    • open its doors with probability 0.2, if they are closed;
    • close its doors with probability 0.2, if they are open;
    • if its doors are closed and it is not on Floor 3, move up one floor leaving its doors closed with probability 0.3;
    • if its doors are closed and it is not on Floor 1, move down one floor leaving its doors closed with probability 0.3;
    • otherwise, remain where it is with its doors as they are.

    (a) What is the probability that the left elevator will be on Floor 1 with its doors open at any clock tick?

    (b) What is the probability that either one or the other of the elevators will be on Floor 1 with its doors open at any clock tick?

(c) What is the probability that both of the elevators will be on Floor 1 with their doors open at any clock tick?

(d) Angela Skule arrives on Floor 1 in front of the elevators at a certain time. She wants to go to the second floor. If an elevator door already has its doors open, she will get in it. If neither elevator has its doors open, she will wait until an elevator arrives and opens its doors, and then get in it. If both elevator doors are open, she will prefer the left one. She will stay on the elevator until it has moved to the second floor and opened its doors, and then get off there. What is the probability of Angela taking k clock ticks to get out of the elevator on the second floor, for $k = 1..20$?

(e) Ralph Skule arrives on Floor 1 at the same time Angela does. Ralph wants to go to the third floor. If an elevator door already has its doors open, Ralph and Angela will both get in it. If neither elevator has its doors open, they will wait until an elevator arrives and opens its doors, and then get in it. If both elevator doors are open, they will prefer the left one. At the 20th clock tick, what is the probability that Angela will still be in the elevator and Ralph has arrived already at the third floor?

3 RECURSION

3.1. INTRODUCTION

Recursion is a technique that is often useful when algorithms are being developed. It is convenient to study it in some detail at this stage. Several examples are included for clarity and to indicate the way the method can be applied in practice.

Recursion can be used to simplify or improve the elegance of algorithms while at the same time often improving their performance. Many algorithms are slow or complicated when represented in a brute-force way. They can become more efficient, less prone to special cases, or more understandable when they are implemented using recursion.

A recursive algorithm is an algorithm that is described in terms of itself. A simplistic but general scenario of a recursive algorithm is the following:

```
function recur ( n: typeOfN ) : typeOfN

    % Find out if the termination
    % condition has been reached
    if ( n is a special case) then
        result ( answer for the special case)
    else
        % Call recur with a subset of the data
        result f2(n) * recur ( f1(n) )
    end if
end recur
```

The scenario shows a quite simple case. The functions f1 and f2 need not be described further. but it is necessary that f1 move n closer to a special case, or at least not further away from one. Eventually, after possibly many recursive calls, the special case will be reached and the recursion will stop. The function f1 would in a practical case relentlessly move the parameter closer to one of the special cases. Because of this effect, a recursive algorithm is one that solves some problem by solving one or more versions of the same problem that are less computationally demanding.

In a real recursive algorithm there might be several recursive calls. Thus, the part of the scenario that does the recursive call is just a rough approximation to what will be found in many algorithms. How often the algorithm calls itself depends on the actual calculation that is being done.

A standard example of a recursive algorithm is Euclid's algorithm to find the greatest common divisor (gcd) of two integers. Call the integers x and y, both greater than zero. Euclid's algorithm is based on the fact that if t is the greatest common divisor of x and y, then t is also a divisor of $x-y$. The gcd t is also a divisor of $x-ky$, where k is an integer. If k is properly chosen, $x-ky = x \bmod y$, so t is the gcd of y and $x \bmod y$. If $x \bmod y = 0$, then y is the gcd of x and y. This can be represented in a function subprogram as follows:

```
% Euclid's Algorithm
% x>0 and y>0 initially
function gcd(x,y:int):int
    if y=0 then
        result x
    else
        result gcd(y, x mod y)
    end if
end gcd
```

This representation of gcd has much to recommend it; it is elegant and it is efficient. As an example of gcd operating, consider the calculation of the greatest common divisor of the pair of integers 20416847 and 1265429. The table shows the successive values of the parameters x and y in the above program.

x	y
20416847	1265429
1265429	169983
169983	75548
75548	18887
18887	0

All recursive algorithms must have a *termination condition*, so that eventually the algorithm will do something other than invoke itself. The termination condition in the scenario with which this section was introduced was a combination of the notions that

(1)   there exist one or more special cases for which the result of the algorithm is known, and

(2)   there exists a scheme for relentlessly approaching one of the special cases, perhaps calculating some intermediate result along the way. Also, additional calculations might be done after the return from the procedure call.

If the algorithm, or the program that represents it, is to be of any general use it must not be able to avoid terminating. Normally, the termination condition is obtained from knowledge of the value of the function at one or two small values of the parameter. When the function is originally called, the parameter is usually much bigger than these special cases, and successive reductions in the value of the parameter in the subsequent recursive calls guarantee that eventually one of the special cases with a known solution will be done. There will be an immediate result for the special case, without a recursive call.

In practice, the only problem with recursive programs is the computational overhead implied by the procedure calls. The term computational overhead means unavoidable computer instructions that must be executed to do the procedure call. It is difficult to construct a compiler that does not have large overheads associated with the calling of a procedure. The overheads are caused by the various actions that are implicit in calling a procedure, such as saving the state of the calling program at the instant of the call and passing parameters. When a called procedure returns from the call, results must be passed to the calling procedure, and the state previously saved must be restored. It is in some cases possible to avoid the overheads when the program that represents the algorithm is written, simply by converting the recursive procedure into a program with a loop in it. Sometimes, it is either not practical or not possible to do this. Usually, some auxiliary data will be required to keep track of the data otherwise associated with each of the recursive calls. Sometimes the program can be designed so this is not necessary.

If the last statement executed in the recursive procedure is the recursive call, the procedure is said to be *tail recursive*. It is easy to make a tail recursive procedure into a non-recursive procedure. It is convenient to refer to one instance of the recursive procedure as the *calling procedure*, and the next instance of the recursive procedure as the *called procedure*. If the procedure is tail recursive, when a return from the called procedure happens, the calling procedure also immediately returns, because by definition the recursive call is the last statement that the calling procedure executes. Thus, in a tail recursive procedure, as soon as the first return happens due to one of the special cases being encountered, there will be a whole sequence of returns bouncing right back to the original call of the procedure.

The scenario that was mentioned at the start of this section is not tail recursive, because after a return from the recursive call the result must be multiplied by `f2(n)`. This product will be done after the return from the recursive call. However, the scenario is tail

recursive for the special case of f2(n) being absent. The scenario
then becomes the following.

```
function recur ( n: typeOfN ) : typeOfN

    % Find out if the termination
    % condition has been reached
    if ( n is a special case) then
        result ( answer for the special case)
    else
        % Call recur with a subset of the data
        result recur ( f1(n) )
    end if
end recur
```

Then, the recursive procedure will behave as if the following
code had been written:

```
function recur ( n: typeOfN ) : typeOfN

    if ( n is a special case) then
        result ( answer for the special case)
    else
        if ( f1(n) is a special case) then
            result ( answer for the special case)
        else
            if ( f1( f1(n) ) is a special case) then
                result ( answer for the special case)
            else       • • •
            end if
        end if
    end if
end recur
```

The non-recursive version of the program can now be written in a
more efficient way. This step may not be easy, but in principle it can
be done, as shown next.

```
function recur ( n: typeOfN ) : typeOfN

    var arg: typeOfN     % will hold the present argument
    arg := n
    loop
        if ( arg is a special case) then
            result ( answer for the special case)
        else
            arg := f1(arg)
        end if
    end loop
end recur
```

The gcd program was tail recursive. It has been converted into
a loop, shown next. From an inspection of the way this has been
done, an instance of the technique is apparent. A non-recursive

version of the gcd program requires one integer of auxiliary data.

```
function gcd(x,y:int):int        %x>0 and y>0 initially
    var t:int
    loop
        exit when y=0
        t:= x mod y
        x:= y
        y:= t
    end loop
    result x
end gcd
```

As another example of recursion, consider the computation of $\cos x$. The best technique is to use a power series that is a good approximation for $\cos x$ for some range of values of x, say $-x_{big} \leq x \leq x_{big}$. This is the technique that is used in the standard library program that you automatically invoke when you write cos(x) in your program. If x happens to be within the range $-x_{big} \leq x \leq x_{big}$, then the power series may be used immediately. But if abs $x > x_{big}$, the argument of the cos function must be somehow reduced to be within the right range.

Since $\cos x = \cos(-x)$, the sign of the argument can be forced to be positive without an error developing. One way to do the reduction is to repeatedly subtract 2π radians from the (forced to be positive) argument. This works because $\cos(x - 2\pi k) = \cos x$ for k any integer. There are two problems with this process. First, a lot of subtractions will be necessary if x is large. This takes time and may introduce numerical errors because what is being done, in effect, is to find the reduced argument by subtracting two large numbers, x and $2\pi k$. In general, the number of subtractions is $O(x)$. Second, there is no guarantee that subtracting $2\pi k$ from x will result in a new argument in the right range. If x_{big} is, say, $\pi/8$, then it would be easy to overshoot and never arrive at the range. It is obvious from simple trigonometry how to recover from this problem, and computing an appropriate k, subtracting $x - 2\pi k$, and then adjusting the angle is usually the best method of reducing to the range of angles suitable for power series evaluation.

A recursive method to reduce the range is interesting as an academic exercise. The way to reduce the range that is given next is not the best way to do it, but it will serve as an example of the use of recursion. It just goes to show that, while recursion is a superb tool that often can be used to simplify and make elegant, it can be misused. With that in mind, a recursive way to do the reduction is to use the identity $\cos x = 2\cos^2 x/2 - 1$.

```
function cos ( x: real) : real

    var arg: real      % argument forced positive
    % Force the argument positive
    arg := abs(x)
    % Find out if the termination
    % condition has been reached
    if ( 0 <= x <= xbig ) then
        result ( value of the power series )
    else
        % Call cos with a reduced range
        result 2.0*cos(0.5*x) - 1.0
    end if
end recur
```

It is not hard to see that the number of recursive calls will be $O(\log_2 x)$. The method can be improved, because from simple but tedious trigonometry $\cos x$ can always be written as a polynomial in $\cos^2 x /(2k)$. The formula used above is for $k = 1$. The rate of convergence to the desired range might be accelerated by using a larger k. For instance,

$$\cos x = 32 \cos^6 \frac{x}{6} - 48 \cos^4 \frac{x}{6} + 18 \cos^2 \frac{x}{6} - 1$$

has $k = 3$, and might increase the rate that the desired range is reached. While it is elegant to describe the recursive method, in practice it would be better to convert it to an equivalent non-recursive method. The fact that there is a better way to reduce the range than the recursive method given above is unusual and demonstrates that no programming technique can be applied without thought and analysis.

In general, recursion is a powerful design tool; it should be used wherever it naturally appears. Its use makes algorithms more elegant and simpler to conceive and to understand. If recursion is likely to be too expensive in a program, it should be removed as part of the programming process, not as part of the algorithm design.

There are many other algorithms that use recursion. *Quicksort*, a technique of sorting an array of data into ascending sequence, is a recursive algorithm. It sorts n objects by recursively calling itself twice, each time to sort $n/2$ objects. Another recursive sorting algorithm called *heapsort* will be studied later. These sorting algorithms are two classical algorithms. Before studying quicksort, it is useful to take a general look at the reason why recursive algorithms are often quicker than the underlying brute-force solution.

3.2. DIVIDE AND CONQUER

The algorithm design technique known as *divide and conquer* can be used for problems in which

(1)   the problem, calculating say someFunction(n), can be solved for all pertinent values of n, and

(2)   there exists a recurrence relation of the form

$$\text{someFunction}(n) = F(\text{ someFunction}(\frac{n}{c})) \ .$$

The idea is to solve the original problem, someFunction(n), by solving the smaller problem $F(\text{ someFunction}(\frac{n}{c}))$. This action can be done recursively, so that the only calculations actually done are the computation of the value for one of the termination conditions, and several nested evaluations of the function F. Thus, divide and conquer depends upon finding a way to solve the original problem by solving a number of identical smaller problems and then applying this technique recursively until the problems become trivial. Any application of divide and conquer is inherently recursive.

    A general analytical analysis of divide and conquer can be done. The problem is set up as follows:

(1)   Suppose that when $n=1$ the problem is known to be solvable in time b (a constant). This is the termination condition for the recursion.

(2)   Instead of solving the original problem dealing with n data objects, it is proposed to deal with only n/c data objects. It is not likely that the rest of the data can be just ignored, so the method will need to deal with more than one group of n/c data objects.

(3)   It will take some computational effort to split the data up into blocks that each contain n/c data objects. This effort will be some function $s(n)$.

    Suppose the original problem can be solved by a applications of an algorithm to blocks of the data each with n/c members. There will be a relationship between $T(n)$ and $T(n/c)$ of the following form:

$$T(1) = b$$

$$T(n) = a \ T(\frac{n}{c}) + s(n) \qquad \text{for} \ \ n > 1$$

    In many cases it will be found that the computational effort to split the data up into blocks with n/c members will be proportional to n. It will be convenient to use $b = T(1)$ as the constant of proportionality. This is an algebraic convenience and is not critical to the analysis. The above relationship with these changes becomes the following.

$$T(1) = b$$

$$T(n) = a\ T(\frac{n}{c}) + bn \qquad \text{for } n > 1$$

Recurrence equations of the form given above are characteristic of the divide and conquer technique. To simplify the solution of this recurrence relation, it is helpful to assume that $n = c^k$ for some integer k. This is done so that the number of variables being dealt with is always exactly divisible by c, or it has been reduced to the special case value 1. This assumption is not necessary, but it avoids the appearance of floor and ceil functions, with their attendant mess and confusion. Applying the recurrence repeatedly,

$$T(n) = aT(\frac{n}{c}) + bn = a\left[aT(\frac{n}{c^2}) + b\frac{n}{c}\right] + bn$$

$$= a^2T(\frac{n}{c^2}) + \frac{a}{c}bn + bn$$

$$= a^3T(\frac{n}{c^3}) + \frac{a^2}{c^2}bn + \frac{a}{c}bn + bn$$

$$= a^{k-1}T(\frac{n}{c^{k-1}}) + bn\sum_{i=0}^{k-2}(\frac{a}{c})^i$$

$$= a^kT(\frac{n}{c^k}) + bn\sum_{i=0}^{k-1}(\frac{a}{c})^i \quad .$$

This can be simplified by using $\frac{n}{c^k} = 1$, $T(1) = b$, and rearranging the first term as follows:

$$a^kT(\frac{n}{c^k}) = a^kT(1) = a^k b = a^k b \frac{n}{c^k} = bn\ (\frac{a}{c})^k \quad .$$

After this change, the first term can be incorporated in the series with a change in the limit of summation, as follows:

$$T(n) = bn\ (\frac{a}{c})^k + bn\sum_{i=0}^{k-1}(\frac{a}{c})^i$$

$$T'(n) = bn \sum_{i=0}^{k} (\frac{a}{c})^i \ .$$

This is a geometric progression, so

$$T(n) = bn \ \frac{1-(\frac{a}{c})^{k+1}}{1-\frac{a}{c}} \ .$$

There are three cases to be considered, depending on whether a is less than, equal to, or greater than, c. Each exhibits characteristic behaviour, and each occurs in practice.

$a < c$ If $a < c$ the term $(\frac{a}{c})^{k+1}$ is small for large enough k, and $T(n) \approx bn \ (1+\frac{a}{c})$. If $a \ll c$, $T(n) \approx bn$. In either case, $T(n)$ is $O(n)$.

$a = c$ This will be the case of interest in many applications of divide and conquer that are covered in this text. If $a = c$, the geometric progression becomes $T(n) = bn \ (k+1)$. But $n = c^k$, so $T(n) = bn \ \log_c n + bn \approx bn \log_c cn$. Hence, for $a = c$, $T(n)$ is $O(n \log n)$.

$a > c$ If $a > c$, then $T(n) \approx bn \ (\frac{a}{c})^k$, and because of the assumption $n = c^h$, $T(n) \approx ba^h = ba^{\log_c n}$. Let $\xi = a^{\log_c n}$. Then taking the logarithm of this equation to base c, $\log_c \xi = (\log_c n)(\log_c a)$ and this gives the result $\log_c \xi = \log_c n^{\log_c a}$, from which we get $\xi = a^{\log_c n} = n^{\log_c a}$. Finally, this collection of logarithmic identities gives $T(n) \approx bn^{\log_c a}$ so that $T(n) = O(n^{\log_c a})$.

Summary of Divide and Conquer	
a versus c	$T(n)$
$a < c$	$O(n)$
$a = c$	$O(n \log n)$
$a > c$	$O(n^{\log_c a})$

If $a < c$, divide and conquer algorithms are remarkably quick. This case rarely happens, because at each step some of the data is being rejected from all consideration; a blocks with n/c members hold fewer than n data elements. The normal case in practice is $a = c$, so that often algorithms that use divide and conquer have complexity

$O(n \log n)$. If $a > c$, the performance of these algorithms is dependent on the exponent $\log_c a$. This case arises occasionally in practice.

3.3. QUICKSORT

all members $< a_j$	a_j	all members $> a_j$

1   j-1 j j+1 n

Often quicksort is the best method of sorting an array *in situ* with very little auxiliary storage required. Quicksort uses divide and conquer to speed up sorting. It selects one of the members of the array and inserts it at the location it will occupy in the sorted array. Let the selected member be a_j. By shuffling the items about, quicksort arranges that all the array members with indexes $< j$ are less than or equal to the selected member. At the same time, using the same shuffle, it also arranges that all the array members with indexes $> j$ are greater than or equal to the selected member. The selected member has been inserted at the correct place. All items with lower index are less than it, and all objects with higher index are greater

---

```
var A: array 1..n of sometype     % the data to be sorted
procedure quicksort( left, right: 1..n )
    % left and right are indexes to the left end and
    % the right end of the (sub)array to be sorted
    var spot: 1..n    % spot will be the location
                      % of the selected object
    % do the select and shuffle
    selectAndShuffle(spot, left, right)
    % quicksort the lower subarray if it has > 1 member
    if spot > left then
        quicksort(left, spot-1)
    end if
    % quicksort the upper subarray if it has > 1 member
    if spot < right
        quicksort(spot+1, right)
    end if
end quicksort
```

Figure 3.1: Quicksort.

---

than it. The items with lower index may now be sorted by recursively
quicksorting them and, similarly, the items with higher index. These
two arrays of items both have fewer than n elements. Ideally, they
both will have about $n/2$ elements.

In principle, then, quicksort operates as shown in Figure 3.1. A
call to `quicksort(1, n)` will sort the array.

```
procedure selectAndShuffle(var here, leftend, rightend: 1..n)
    var Bot, Top: 1..n      %Bot is the leftmost object
                            %Top is the rightmost object
    var UDsw: string(4) := "DecT"    % Which way to shuffle
            % "DecT" --> decrement Top
            % "IncB" --> increment Bot
    Bot := leftend
    Top := rightend
    loop
        exit when Top <= Bot
        if UDsw = 'DecT'
        then
            if A(Top) < A(Bot)
            then
                Interchange(Top,Bot)
                UDsw := 'IncB'
                Bot += 1
            else
                Top -= 1
            end if
        else
            if A(Top) < A(Bot)
            then
                Interchange(Top,Bot)
                UDsw := 'DecT'
                Top -= 1
            else
                Bot += 1
            end if
        end if
    end loop
    % return the spot found
    here := Bot
end selectAndSuffle
```

Figure 3.2: selectAndShuffle.

The only remaining aspect of quicksort is `selectAndShuffle`. There are many ways that this can be done, and consequently many slightly different versions of quicksort. The method used here and shown in Figure 3.2 is one of the simplest versions of `selectAndShuffle`. It is almost as effective as many much more elaborate versions.

The code in Figure 3.2 shows that `selectAndShuffle` compares the two end objects, A_{left} and A_{right} and swaps them if $A_{left} > A_{right}$. If a swap is not necessary, either the left index is incremented or the right index is decremented, and the comparison is repeated. The procedure starts with the right index being

A_1	A_2	A_3	A_4	A_5	A_6	A_7	A_8	A_9	A_{10}
B6	10	4	16	5	11	2	8	1	T9
B6	10	4	16	5	11	2	8	T1	9
1	B10	4	16	5	11	2	8	T6	9
1	B6	4	16	5	11	2	T8	10	9
1	B6	4	16	5	11	T2	8	10	9
1	2	B4	16	5	11	T6	8	10	9
1	2	4	B16	5	11	T6	8	10	9
1	2	4	B6	5	T11	16	8	10	9
1	2	4	B6	T5	11	16	8	10	9
1	2	4	5	BT6	11	16	8	10	9
B1	2	4	T5	**6**	11	16	8	10	9
B1	2	T4	5	**6**	11	16	8	10	9
B1	T2	4	5	**6**	11	16	8	10	9
BT1	2	4	5	**6**	11	16	8	10	9
1	B2	4	T5	**6**	11	16	8	10	9
1	B2	T4	5	**6**	11	16	8	10	9
1	BT2	4	5	**6**	11	16	8	10	9
1	**2**	B4	T5	**6**	11	16	8	10	9
1	**2**	BT4	5	**6**	11	16	8	10	9
1	**2**	**4**	**5**	**6**	B11	16	8	10	T9
1	**2**	**4**	**5**	**6**	9	B16	8	10	T11
1	**2**	**4**	**5**	**6**	9	B11	8	T10	16
1	**2**	**4**	**5**	**6**	9	10	B8	T11	16
1	**2**	**4**	**5**	**6**	9	10	8	BT11	16
1	**2**	**4**	**5**	**6**	B9	10	T8	**11**	**16**
1	**2**	**4**	**5**	**6**	8	B10	T9	**11**	**16**
1	**2**	**4**	**5**	**6**	8	BT9	10	**11**	**16**
1	**2**	**4**	**5**	**6**	**8**	**9**	**10**	**11**	**16**

Table 3.1: Quicksort Example.

Array members that have been moved to the correct site in the array are shown in bold type. The positions of Bot and Top in the selectAndShuffle procedure are shown by prefixing the array entry with a B or a T.

dccremented, and each time a swap is done it alternates between incrementing the left index and decrementing the right index. At the end, the original A_{left} will have been moved to the position it should occupy in the sorted array, and `selectAndShuffle` will return an index to the place in the array at which the original A_{left} has ended up. The index is returned through the parameter `here`. The original A_{left} is the member of the array that has been selected.

Better methods of selecting the array member to be moved to the correct sorted location are known. Sorts based on these methods are somewhat better, but the principle is the same. They often have names such as quickersort, quickestsort, etc.

It is difficult to contrive an effective example of quicksort that demonstrates both its strengths and its weaknesses. The example of Table 3.1 shows the quicksort algorithm sorting an array of integers. With the data in the order given here, quicksort is quite effective in sorting the upper half of the data, but rather less so with the lower half. This is one of the characteristics of quicksort. It is very quick sorting data that is in random order at the start, and rather less efficient for some other starting orders.

3.3.1. Analysis of Quicksort

The case where the selected member is inserted in the middle of the array, so that the two remaining subarrays are both about $n/2$ items long, is the best case and one of the easiest to analyze. The array of n elements is partitioned into one selected element in the correct position, and two subarrays of about $n/2$ elements.

One call to `selectAndShuffle` will take O(`left-right`) comparisons and interchanges. This will always be equal to or less than O(n) operations. Hence, applying the general solution to divide and conquer with $a = c$,

$$T(n) = 2T(\frac{n}{2}) + kn = O(n \log_2 n) \quad .$$

The major weakness of quicksort is in the selection of the element to be correctly sited. In the worst case, if the smallest (or the largest) is the one selected, it will be moved to one of the ends of the array. The array of n elements will be partitioned into one element in the correct position, and a subarray of $n-1$ elements. This effect was seen in the example. If this case happens every time there is a selection,

$$T(n) = T(n-1) + n - 1 = \frac{n(n-1)}{2} = O(n^2) \; .$$

Splitting the array into (roughly) equally sized subarrays (sub-problems) is important. The algorithm given above will, unfortunately, sort an array of already ordered data items in time $O(n^2)$, because it always moves the original a_{left} to the correct position, and a_{left} is already in the correct position. Similar behaviour occurs with an array in exactly the wrong order.

In spite of this flaw, which more elaborate implementations try to overcome, quicksort is one of the best sorts available for data that is not initially ordered in an unfortunate way.

3.4. EXERCISES

1. Modify the gcd function so that it will cope if x or y are initially zero or negative. The complexity of gcd is rather difficult to calculate, but do your changes affect the complexity this algorithm?

2. An array a, declared as shown, contains the coefficients of a polynomial in x:

       var a: array 0..n of real

   Develop an algorithm suitable for a function subprogram to evaluate the polynomial for any x and to return the result. Your algorithm should compute

   $$a_n x^n + a_{n-1} x^{n-1} + \cdots + a_1 x + a_0 \; .$$

   If all arithmetic operations on real numbers take the same computational effort, find the complexity of your algorithm.

   Another way to compute the value of the polynomial is to compute

   $$x \, (x \, (x \, (x \, (x \, \cdots \, (a_n x + a_{n-1}) + a_{n-2}) + \cdots + a_2) + a_1) + a_0 \; .$$

   Develop another algorithm to compute the value of the polynomial, and find its complexity. Compare the two algorithms.

3. Consider the problem of finding both the maximum member and the minimum member of an array A, declared as follows:

       var A: array 0..n of integer

   A simple way to do this is to assume that the first element is both the maximum and the minimum, and then to compare each of the other elements with the maximum and minimum found so far. If a new maximum or minimum is found, it replaces the value found so far. Write a program that works this way, and find its complexity.

   Another way to find the maximum and the minimum is to use divide and conquer. Find the maximum and minimum of both the upper half and the lower half of the array. Compare these values to find the maximum and minimum of the whole array. Clearly, this process can be applied recursively to find the maximum and minimum of the upper and lower halves of the array. The termination case is the finding of the maximum and minimum of a single element. Write a program that would work this way, and find its complexity.

   How many recursive calls would be involved in the second algorithm? Which program is preferable?

4. Assume that a power series to calculate $\sin x$ for $-\pi/8 \leq x \leq \pi/8$ is known. It is desirable to use this series to calculate both $\sin x$ and $\cos x$. Compare the recursive method given in the text to reduce the value of x to this range with the subtraction method discussed. Work out the complexity of both cases.

5. In the analysis of divide and conquer, it was assumed that $s(n) = bn$. Show that the choice of b as the constant of proportionality makes little difference in the result.

6. In the analysis of divide and conquer, it was assumed that $s(n) = bn$. Repeat the analysis if $s(n) = kn^2$.

7. In the selectAndShuffle procedure, the element of the array that was selected was always the leftmost one. Consider the case in which the element to be selected is chosen at random from the (sub)array to be sorted. This could be done by choosing an element at random, swapping it with the leftmost, and using the program shown in the text. Analyze the performance of the modified algorithm. For the method given in the text there is an known poor order for the initial array to be in. Is this true for the changed algorithm?

8. Two arrays A and B, declared as shown, contain the coefficients of two polynomials in x.

```
var A,B: array 0..n of real
```

A_j and B_j contain the coefficient of x^j for their corresponding polynomial. Develop an algorithm to multiply these two polynomials, with the answer appearing in another array C. This problem can be solved by divide and conquer. For ease of analysis, let the number of coefficients in each polynomial be a power of two. Split each polynomial into an upper half and a lower half. The upper half will have a common factor of some power of x. With this hint, develop a divide and conquer multiply algorithm, analyze it, and compare its performance with the algorithm you first developed.

9. Find the complexity of gcd. (The mathematical operations involved in answering this question can be complicated. Try to find some simplifying tactic, and reason about its general applicability.)

4 RECURSIVE DATA TYPES

4.1. INTRODUCTION

In Chapters 2 and 3, it was shown that recursion is of great value in planning an algorithm. Recursion can also be used to great advantage in the design of data structures. It makes the interdependencies of the data elements explicit, and can greatly simplify program logic.

4.2. COLLECTIONS

A data structure called a *collection* will be of considerable use in representing dynamic data types such as trees, which are an important part of this course. A collection can be thought of as an aggregation of objects, any member of which is selectable at runtime with a *pointer*. Usually each object is a record. These objects may be dynamically created and destroyed at runtime. A doubly-linked

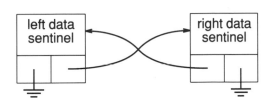

Figure 4.1: An Empty Collection.

(forward and backward) linear list of data aggregates of identical form can be constructed with a collection of records.

In Figure 4.1 the arrangement of pointers is shown with arrows. The collections are modelled with rectangles. This structure is shown in the following code segment:

```
1     var list: collection of node
2     type node:
3         record
4             contents: elementsOfTheNode
5             forwardPointer: pointer to list
6             backwardPointer: pointer to list
7         end record

8     var leftmost: pointer to list
9     var rightmost: pointer to list

      % create the leftmost data sentinel
10    new list,leftmost
11    list(leftmost).contents:= leftmostDataSentinel

      % create the rightmost data sentinel
12    new list,rightmost
13    list(rightmost).contents:= rightmostDataSentinel

      % point from the leftmost to the proper things
14    list(leftmost).backwardPointer:= nil(list)
15    list(leftmost).forwardPointer:= rightmost

      % point from the rightmost to the proper things
16    list(rightmost).backwardPointer:= leftmost
17    list(rightmost).forwardPointer:= nil(list)
```

Individual new members of the aggregate easily can be created and destroyed. Line 1 of this code declares list to be a collection of node. Lines 2 through 7 declare the node form. The elementsOfTheNode are the data that is contained in the node. The actual form of this data is not relevant to the construction of the recursive data type but is associated with the (unknown) algorithm that is going to use the data. The backwardPointer will point to the logically previous element of the list, while the forward-Pointer will point to the logically next element of the list. Lines 8 and 9 declare leftmost and rightmost to be pointers to elements of the collection list. They will be assigned values in Lines 10 and 12 when these elements are created. Line 10 creates the leftmost element of the list and assigns a value to the pointer leftmost.

It is good programming practice to terminate each end of a list with an easily recognized sentinel element. Doing so often simplifies programming logic by eliminating many special cases and tests. This is being done here. The elementsOfTheNode are assigned some

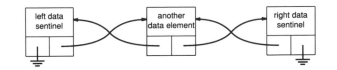

Figure 4.2: A Collection with One Member.

sentinel value `leftmostDataSentinel` in Line 11. Lines 12 and 13 create the `rightmost` element of the list in a similar way. Lines 14 and 15 assign values to the `backwardPointer` and the `forward-Pointer` of the `leftmost` element of the list. The `backward-Pointer` is set to the `nil` pointer value for this collection, because there is no element of the `list` to the left of the `leftmost` one. The `forwardPointer` points to the `rightmost` element, because there are no intermediate elements in the `list`. Lines 16 and 17 assign values to the `backwardPointer` and the `forwardPointer` of the `rightmost` element of the list. The `forwardPointer` is set to the `nil` pointer value for this collection, because there is no element of the `list` to the right of the `rightmost` one. The `backward-Pointer` points to the `leftmost` element.

```
1      var another: pointer to list

       % create the list element to be added
2      new list,another
3      list(another).contents:= realContents

       % put the proper pointer values in the new element
4      list(another).backwardPointer:= leftmost
5      list(another).forwardPointer:= rightmost

       % include the new element by changing pointers
       % to point to the new element
6      list(leftmost).forwardPointer:= another
7      list(rightmost).backwardPointer:= another
```

Having set the list up in this way, it is simple to add a new element to it. The structure is shown in Figure 4.2. The code to accomplish the insertion of a new element in the list is given above. Line 1 declares `another` to be a pointer to an element of list. Line 2 creates a new element and assigns to the pointer another a value that will be used in locating this new element. Line 3 inserts the contents (not a sentinel this time) in the node. Lines 4 and 5 set up the backward pointer and forward pointer of the newly created list element, so they correctly indicate its intended place in the list. Lines 6 and 7 change the forward pointer of the leftmost element and the backward pointer of the rightmost element to point at the new element. This new element is now inserted in the list.

The sentinels should be chosen so that there is an ordering relation < such that, for all possible *realContents*,

```
leftmostDataSentinel < realContents < rightmostDataSentinel
```

This will permit comparisons between the contents and the sentinels without worry about errors or surprises. If this method is not possible because no suitable sentinels can be found, it will be necessary to detect the end of the list by examining the pointer to the next element to see if it has the value nil. The need to do this will often require a lot of extra code, and will sometimes result in some complicated decision-making that it would be better to avoid.

The order in which the pointers were assigned values when the new data element was added to the list is a matter of good programming practice. It is best to get the element completely set up for insertion into the list, and then finally adjust the pointers in the list to include it. Inserting the element into the list first tends to be error-prone, and in some special situations may be unsafe.

When an element is no longer required, the space it occupies can be recovered with the free statement. Care must be taken to ensure that no use will be made of any pointers that point to an element that has been freed. These pointers are said to be *dangling* and are a common source of error.

4.3. PERMUTATIONS, QUEUES, AND STACKS

Queues and *stacks* are a useful prelude to the study of recursive data structures. The capabilities implied by algorithms that use queues and stacks will be needed in understanding the recursive structures. It will be seen that neither a queue nor a stack is a recursive data structure in its own right. Nevertheless, they are included here because it is here that they are first needed.

A *permutation* of n objects is an arrangement of them in a distinct order. There are $n!$ distinct permutations of n objects. If the original list is

```
        a b c d e f g h i j k l m ,
```
then each of the following sequences is a permutation:
```
        a b c d e f g h i j k l m
        e j b f l h d a c g m k i
        m l k j i h g f e d c b a
```
The elementary operations associated with a data structure are the insertion and deletion of data into it and out of it. A sequence of elementary operations will produce a permutation on the input data as it moves into the data structure and then out of it. The study of the nature of these permutations that can be achieved with a data structure is important. It indicates a fundamental property of the data structure that indicates what sort of structure to use in other algorithms.

4.3.1. Permutations with a Queue

A *queue* is a list of data objects in a sequence, that, like all lists, has two ends. For purposes of reference, these are called the left end and the right end. The left end is sometimes called the input end and the right end is sometimes called the output end. New objects are always put in at the left end, and the output of an object is always from the right end. This gives the effect of first-in, first-out, so a queue is sometimes called a *FIFO structure*. Queues are often used as storage for data or operations that must be performed later, where order is significant.

Objects input to a queue can appear at the output only in the same order that they were put in it. The queue cannot generate another permutation of its input, regardless of the order in which insertion into and deletion from the queue are done. For example, let the input be 1, 2, 3 and 4, in that order. Let I represent insertion, and let D represent deletion. Then certain sequences of 4 I's and 4 D's represent all objects moving through the queue. For example, the sequence I D I I D I D D will result in the queue contents evolving as follows:

Operation	Start	I	D	I	I	D	I	D	D
queue contents	empty	1	-	2	3 2	3	4 3	4	-

The output that results from these operations is the same sequence as the input.

Difficulties arise if the queue is stored in an indexed linear list. Starting at location zero, successive insertions will occur at locations zero, one, two, three, and so on. Deletions will start at location zero, then one, etc. Table 4.1 shows this effect happening for a queue that is initially empty.

The queue appears to "walk" through memory. That is, the queue appears to move up the indexed linear list as successive insertions and deletions occur. When the last entry in the list is occupied, subsequent insertions must not extend beyond the list, and the queue must "wrap around" to location zero, which makes program logic tricky.

If the data elements to be placed in the queue are complicated, it may be advantageous to use a recursive data type in a doubly linked list to store the data. However, the queue may not contain the data at all. It is common to have the queue contain pointers to the actual data. The advantage of doing this is obvious. Not only are all queue elements identical in size, but the entire data element need not actually be assembled until it is actually about to be manipulated. Sometimes this last feature is quite helpful in algorithm design.

4.3.2. Permutations with a Stack

A *stack* is a list of data objects in which input and output are both done at the same end (called the *top* of the stack). The stack is also said to have a *bottom*, that coincides with the top when one entry is in the stack. A stack is a last-in, first-out, or a *LIFO structure*, and can produce many permutations.

Table 4.1: A Queue in Memory.								
0	1	2	3	4	5	6	7	8
a								
a	b							
a	b	c						
	b	c						
	b	c	d					
		c	d					
		c	d	e				
			d	e				

Table 4.2: Permutations with a Stack.	
Permutation	Sequence of Operations
123	S X S X S X
132	S X S S X X
213	S S X X S X
231	S S X S X X
312	not possible
321	S S S X X X

Let S represent insertion, which is often called *PUSH*. Let X represent removal, called *POP*. Certain sequences of n S's and n X's produce a new permutation of the input objects. Let the input be 1, 2 and 3 in that order. The permutations and the operation sequences shown in Table 4.2 are equivalent.

To be *admissible* the sequence of operations must have n S's and n X's, and the number of S's done at any point in the sequence must not be smaller than the number of X's. All the above sequences are admissible. The sequence XSSSXX is not admissible. One can't remove (POP) an object not yet inserted (PUSHED). The sequence SXXSSX is not admissible, either.

4.3.2.1. Unachievability Condition
A permutation cannot be achieved with a stack if, in order to obtain the output in the desired order, an item in the stack that is not on the top would have to be popped. See the example above, where 312 was not obtainable. For 3 to be first popped, 1 then 2 must be stacked, and 1 cannot be removed before 2.

In general it is possible to obtain the permutation $p_1 p_2 p_3 ... p_n$ from 1 2 3...n using a stack if and only if there are no indices $i < j < k$ such that $p_j < p_k < p_i$. For the 312 case, $i = 1$, $j = 2$, $k = 3$ and $(p_j = 1) < (p_k = 2) < (p_i = 3)$.

4.3.2.2. Achievable Permutations
There are n! permutations in total. Each permutation that a stack can do is identifiable with a unique sequence of n S's and n X's. There are $\begin{bmatrix} 2n \\ n \end{bmatrix}$ distinct combinations of n S's and n X's, but not all are

admissible. If A is the number of inadmissible sequences, then the number of permutations M_n achievable with a stack is

$$M_n = \binom{2n}{n} - A \ .$$

To obtain A, consider an arbitrary inadmissible sequence Λ_x. If it has n S's and n X's, it must have the form

$$\Lambda_x = \Lambda_a X \Lambda_b \ .$$

Λ_a is an admissible sequence having m S's and m X's, for $0 \le m < n$, and Λ_b is a sequence of $n - m$ S's and $n - m - 1$ X's.

Define $\overline{\Lambda}_x = \overline{\Lambda}_a S \Lambda_b$. $\overline{\Lambda}_x$ is obtained by

(1)   changing the X that makes Λ_x inadmissible to an S.
(2)   changing all X's in Λ_a to S's and all S's in Λ_a to X's to form $\overline{\Lambda}_a$.

For example:

$$\Lambda_x = S \, X \, X \, S \, S \, X$$

$$\overline{\Lambda}_x = X \, S \, S \, S \, S \, X$$

It is evident that $\overline{\Lambda}_x$ must have $n + 1$ S's and $n - 1$ X's. Any sequence of $n + 1$ S's and $n - 1$ X's is a $\overline{\Lambda}_x$ corresponding to a unique inadmissible Λ_x. This is because the process of forming $\overline{\Lambda}_x$ can be reversed to regenerate Λ_x and clearly the Λ_x will not be admissible.

An example is given for $n = 3$ in Table 4.3. The input is assumed to be 1 2 3 in that order. The output for admissible sequences of sequences of three S's and three X's is shown. If the sequence is inadmissible, $\overline{\Lambda}_x$ is given.

There are $\binom{2n}{n-1}$ sequences of $n + 1$ S's and $n - 1$ X's. Hence the number of permutations of n objects achievable with a stack is:

$$M_n = \binom{2n}{n} - \binom{2n}{n-1} = \frac{1}{n+1} \binom{2n}{n} \ .$$

For the above example, the results are the following:

$$\binom{6}{3} = 20 \ \text{ and } \ \binom{6}{2} = 15 \ \text{ so } \ M_3 = \binom{6}{3} - \binom{6}{2} = 5 \ .$$

Stacks are widely used in algorithms. There is a very close relationship between a stack and the data space in memory needed to calculate an expression. Also, programs have data associated with procedures. Most modern programming languages implicitly assume that this data is allocated on a stack when the procedure is called.

Table 4.3: Example of Permutations with a Stack.	
Sequence	Output
1. S S S X X X	OUTPUT = 321
2. S S X S X X	OUTPUT = 231
3. S S X X S X	OUTPUT = 213
4. S S X X X S	X X S S S S 1.
5. S X S S X X	OUTPUT = 132
6. S X S X S X	OUTPUT = 123
7. S X S X X S	X S X S S S 2.
8. S X X X S S	X S S X S S 3.
9. S X X S X S	X S S S X S 4.
10. S X X S S X	X S S S S X 5.
11. X S S S X X	S S S S X X 6.
12. X S S X S X	S S S X S X 7.
13. X S S X X S	S S S X X S 8.
14. X S X X S S	S S X X S S 9.
15. X S X S X S	S S X S X S 10.
16. X S X S S X	S S X S S X 11.
17. X X X S S S	S X X S S S 12.
18. X X S X S S	S X S X S S 13.
19. X X S S X S	S X S S X S 14.
20. X X S S S X	S X S S S X 15.

4.4. BINARY SEARCH TREES

A *binary search tree* is a structure widely used to store data in many diverse applications. It is found in compilers, and it is frequently used in algorithms dealing with variable length data objects. In most of these new data may appear at any time, or some of the data may disappear.

A binary search tree is composed of nodes containing

(1)   some information (or the equivalent),

(2)   a left pointer to a possibly empty left subtree, and

(3)   a right pointer to a possibly empty right subtree.

A *parent* node has two children, a *left child* and a *right child*, either of which may be empty. One of the nodes is the *root node*. Every tree node except the root has exactly one parent. The root is the common ancestor of all the nodes in the tree. A node that has null left and right pointers is called a *leaf*. In a tree, it is forbidden for any child to have two parents.

For a tree to be useful, there must be an algorithm to determine whether the data in some node corresponds to some particular sought-for data and, if so, which node it is. A simple and almost universally used algorithm can be described in three steps. Starting at the root:

(1)   Compare the sought-for data with the node data. If they are equal, the sought-for data is in the node being examined.

(2)   If the sought-for data is less than the node data, the node containing the sought-for data should be in the left subtree of the node being examined. That is, the data in all the nodes in the left subtree will be *less than* the information in the node being examined. Make the left child of the node being examined the new node to be examined. If the node being examined has no left child, the sought-for data can be inserted as a new left child of the node being examined if it is desired to add it to the tree.

(3)   If the sought-for data is greater than the node data, the node containing the sought-for data should be in the right subtree of the node being examined. That is, the data in all the nodes in the right subtree will be *greater than* the information in the node being examined. Make the right child of the node being examined the new node to be examined. If the node being examined has no right child, the sought-for data can be inserted as a new right child of the node being examined if it is desired to add it to the tree.

The example tree shown in Figure 4.3, in which it is assumed that $A < B < C < D \cdots < H$ shows the effect of following this procedure.

A location in the tree that corresponds to a node having no left child or having no right child is called an *insertion point*. A new node to be added to the tree will be inserted at one of these points. The insertion point that is used is the first one encountered in an unsuccessful search for that data. A tree with n nodes will always have $n+1$ insertion points. Adding a node adds two new insertion points and removes the one where the new node is attached to the tree. The empty tree has one insertion point. A one node tree has two insertion points, and so on. By induction, starting with the empty tree as a basis and adding nodes successively, it will easily be seen that an n node has $n+1$ insertion points.

Often the data stored in a tree is very complicated, and it is inconvenient to compare the sought-for data with the entire node data. In other cases, the data in the node is much more complete than the sought-for data. This is the case, for instance, when the sought-for data is, for example, a person's name or licence number,

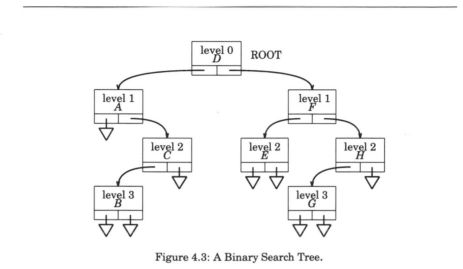

Figure 4.3: A Binary Search Tree.

and the data in the node is a compilation of information about the person. The sought-for data is called the *key*. Corresponding to the data in each node there is a node key to compare with the sought-for key. For efficiency reasons it is usual to store the key with the data.

For example, in the Province of Ontario, each (legal) vehicle driver has a driver's licence number. It is constructed from the first letter of his or her surname, eight more digits that are derived from the rest of his or her name, followed by a six digit coding of his or her birthdate. The sequence T4528 33804 40517 is a possibly legitimate licence number for someone whose surname begins with a T and who was born on May 17, 1944. The authorities can use this data as a key to look up in a tree of data about vehicle drivers any information about the driving record of the individual with that licence number. It is certain that the data in the tree node corresponding to each licenced driver will be much more complete than just the key. It will contain his or her address, the expiration date and type of the licence, some personal physical data like sex, height, and weight, as well as information resulting from bad driving habits.

So far, it has been assumed that the information to be stored in the tree is stored in some node of the tree, and that each node stores some information. A slightly different approach is to use the tree as an *index tree*, in which the information is not stored in the tree at all,

---

```
% declare the structure of the tree and its nodes
var tree: collection of node

type pervasive node:
    record
        contents: typeOfElementsOfTheNode
        leftChildPointer: pointer to tree
        RightChildPointer: pointer to tree
    end record
```

Figure 4.4: The Declaration of the Tree Structure.

---

but in some separate data structure. The pointers of the tree that are not being used to point to subtrees can be used to point to an entry in that separate data structure. The nodes in the tree contain the keys that serve to define a path from the root to the entry in the separate data structure that points to the desired data. Index trees are particularly useful when data needs to be indexed several ways, or when the space that the data occupies can expand or shrink.

In an index tree, the regime of *less than follow the left link* and *greater than follow the right link* that is found in information-carrying trees must be modified. In an index tree, when the sought-for key is equal to the key stored in the node the data has not been found. The data is found only when a leaf of the tree has been encountered. In an index tree, the regime is modified to be *less than* or equal to *follow the left link*. A search of an index tree will eventually arrive at what would be a null pointer in an information-storing tree. This location is used to indicate where one data element is actually stored. Some scheme must be provided to distinguish tree links from those used to point to data. Usually a boolean variable is associated with each pointer to do this.

4.4.1. Tree Search

Trees are searched starting at the root and progressing down the tree, taking the path to the left subtree or the right subtree depending on whether the data being searched for is less than, equal to, or greater than the data in the node. Often, the search procedure is combined with an insertion procedure, so that if the data being searched for is not in the tree, it can be inserted as soon as this fact is discovered.

```
procedure search (element: typeOfElementsOfTheNode,
           var currentNode: pointer to tree)
    % start at the root, a sentinel node with a huge element,
    % whose leftChildPointer points to the actual tree.
    % This has been set up in advance, elsewhere.
    currentNode := root
    loop
        % compare element with the contents of the node
        if element = tree(currentNode).contents
        then
            return         % answer node pointed to by currentNode
        elsif element < tree(currentNode).contents
        then
            % this path taken when comparing with the root
            if tree(currentNode).leftChildPointer = nil(tree)
            then
                % make new node ptd to by left child
                insertNewNode(currentNode, true, element)
                return
            else
                % follow the left subtree
                currentNode := tree(currentNode).leftChildPointer
            end if
        else
            % element > tree(currentNode).contents
            if tree(currentNode).rightChildPointer = nil(tree)
            then
                % make new node ptd to by right child
                insertNewNode(currentNode, false, element)
                return
            else
                % follow the right subtree
                currentNode := tree(currentNode).rightChildPointer
            end if
        end if
    end loop
end search
```

Figure 4.5: The Tree Search Algorithm.

The code shown in Figures 4.4, 4.5, and 4.6 implements the tree search as described above. The root of the tree is pointed to by the variable root. The nodes in the tree are members of the collection tree. It is assumed the elementsOfTheNode can be compared as if they were numbers. If this is not so additional code will be required.

The code in the figures is for an information-storing tree. If the tree is an index tree, some modifications will be required. The search procedure that is shown is not recursive, even though both the information structure and the basic process are recursive. This is done to improve the performance of the search.

4.4.2. Traversing Trees

An orderly method of examining the data in each node of a tree is called a *transversal* of the tree. At any node, there are three things to be done:

(1)   "Visit" the Node (VN). This means doing whatever is to be done at the node, such as printing the information in the node.

(2)   Traverse the left subtree (TLST). If the left subtree is empty this step terminates immediately.

```
% invent a new node when the element is not in the tree
% this procedure is called by search
procedure insertNewNode (var currentNode: pointer to tree,
                             left: boolean,
                             element: typeOfElementsOfTheNode)

    var another: pointer to tree

    new tree,another
    tree(another).contents:= element
    tree(another).leftChildPointer:= nil(tree)
    tree(another).rightChildPointer:= nil(tree)

    % insert the new node in the tree
    if left = true        %left or right side of currentNode
    then
        tree(currentNode).leftChildPointer:= another
    else
        tree(currentNode).rightChildPointer:= another
    end if

    % point at the new node
    currentNode:= another
end insertNewNode
```

Figure 4.6: Inserting a New Node.

---

(3)   Traverse the right subtree (TRST). If the right subtree is
       empty this step terminates immediately.

The order in which these are done at a node changes the nature
of the traversal. There are three traversals that are well known and
are often referred to by name. These are:

Traversal	First Action	Second Action	Third Action
Inorder	TLST	VN	TRST
Preorder	VN	TLST	TRST
Postorder	TLST	TRST	VN

For an example, refer to the tree in Figure 4.3. Writing the nodes
down in the order they are visited, the traversals visit the nodes as
shown in Table 4.4.

Table 4.4: Traversals of Figure 4.3.								
Inorder	A	B	C	D	E	F	G	H
Preorder	D	A	C	B	F	E	H	G
Postorder	B	C	A	E	G	H	F	D

An inorder traversal of a tree sorts the information in the nodes.
The other two traversals have application in the representation of
arithmetic expressions. This aspect of traversals will be studied next.

4.4.3. Polish Expressions

Consider an expression built with only *infix* operators. An infix
operator is the familiar kind, written with two operands separated by
an operator. Typical examples of infix operators are $1+2$ and 3×4.
The tree shown in Figure 4.7 can represent this kind of operator
usage.

There is an obvious way to build a tree to represent an expression that includes only infix operators and variables. For example,
the expression $(a + b /c)*(d - e*f)$ gives the tree shown in Figure
4.8. The results of traversing this tree are:

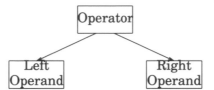

Figure 4.7: An Infix Operator Structure.

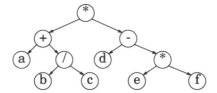

Figure 4.8: An Example Expression Tree.

Preorder   * + a / b c - d * e f

Inorder   a + b / c * d - e * f

Postorder   a b c / + d e f * - *

A pre(post)order traversal of an expression tree yields a sequence known as a pre(post)order expression, while the inorder traversal has merely stripped out the parentheses. Pre(Post)order expressions don't need parentheses to show operator precedence. This feature makes these expressions (particularly postorder) attractive for use in computers. A pre(post)order expression is uniquely related to the corresponding infix expression and a distinct tree. A rearrangement of the tree, taking advantage of commutative operations like $a + b = b + a$, will result in a different traversal and a different expression. The rules that allow rearrangements are the rules of ordinary arithmetic.

A postorder expression is evaluated with the aid of a stack. The objects in the expression are scanned from left to right. If the object is a data reference (a value or the location of a data value) the data value is pushed onto the stack. If the object is an operator, the operator is applied to the top two entries on the stack, and the result is pushed onto the stack. For example, $(2 \times 1 \times 3 + 7 - 9) \times 2$, which has a value of 8, corresponds to the postorder expression [2][1]×[3]×[7]+[9]−[2]×, in which the quantities in brackets represent data values. The stack contents will evolve as follows:

Stack	Rest of Expression	action
empty	[2] [1] × [3] × [7] + [9] − [2] ×	push
[2]	[1] × [3] × [7] + [9] − [2] ×	push
[2] [1]	× [3] × [7] + [9] − [2] ×	×
[2]	[3] × [7] + [9] − [2] ×	push
[2] [3]	× [7] + [9] − [2] ×	×
[6]	[7] + [9] − [2] ×	push
[6] [7]	+ [9] − [2] ×	+
[13]	[9] − [2] ×	push
[13] [9]	− [2] ×	−
[4]	[2] ×	push
[4] [2]	×	×
[8]	*empty*	*halt*

If the expression is rearranged to be $(7 + 3 \times 2 \times 1 - 9) \times 2$, the corresponding postorder expression is [7][3][2]×[1]×+[9]−[2]× and the calculation will proceed as follows:

Stack	Rest of Expression	action
empty	[7] [3] [2] × [1] × + [9] − [2] ×	push
[7]	[3] [2] × [1] × + [9] − [2] ×	push
[7] [3]	[2] × [1] × + [9] − [2] ×	push
[7] [3] [2]	× [1] × + [9] − [2] ×	×
[7] [6]	[1] × + [9] − [2] ×	push
[7] [6] [1]	× + [9] − [2] ×	×
[7] [6]	+ [9] − [2] ×	+
[13]	[9] − [2] ×	push
[13] [9]	− [2] ×	−
[4]	[2] ×	push
[4] [2]	×	×
[8]	*empty*	*halt*

In this case, the stack needs more space to hold temporarily more data objects than it did in the previous case. The depth of the stack may be connected with some cost. Often in a computer, the top few elements in the stack are actually kept in a high speed register. The fact that different representations of the same calculation use different stack depths is a significant factor. In practice, the top of the stack might be kept in registers for added performance, and the number of registers that are available for this service is usually severely limited. The number of registers is small because they are expensive. Compilers that optimize the code that they produce will be sensitive to this kind of issue, as well as many other things.

Operators that take a single operand can be handled by treating them as special two-operand operators that always take a null left operand. If operators that take a single operand are to be used, care must be taken to distinguish the two operand – from the one operand –. This can be done by inventing a special symbol for the latter. Most arithmetic languages also have a one operand + that must be treated similarly.

4.4.4. Analysis of Trees
Trees are probably the most common recursive data structure. It is important that a software engineer be fully aware of their effect on the performance of the algorithms that use them. Unfortunately, some of the analyses are approximate. In general, however, it is astonishing how accuratly the results reflect actuality. The analysis will be done for the case of the information-storing tree. Index trees can easily be analysed in similar ways. The only significant difference in the analysis is that a search of an index tree always terminates at a leaf. The search of an information-storing tree may terminate at an interior node if that is where the information is stored.

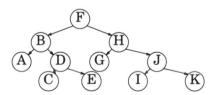

Figure 4.9: A Minimum-Level Tree.

4.4.4.1. *Minimum Number of Levels*

Let n be the number of nodes in a tree. Every node in a tree has either two children, one child, or no children. A tree constructed such that all levels except the highest numbered level are full is called a *minimum level tree*. A minimum level tree is shown in Figure 4.9. Further, if this highest numbered level is full, the tree is a *full tree*. A full tree appears in Figure 4.10.

All nodes in a minimum level tree that are not in the two highest numbered levels will always have two children. In a full tree, all nodes except those in the highest numbered level have two children. The difference between the two is that the full tree has all node positions at all its levels fully populated. A minimum level tree does not have quite enough nodes to do this.

In any tree with the minimum number of levels,

$$
\begin{array}{ccc}
 & 0 & 2^0 \\
 & 1 & 2^1 \\
 & 2 & 2^2 \\
\text{at level} & 3 & 2^3 \\
 & \cdot & \cdot \\
 & \cdot & \cdot \\
 & \cdot & \cdot \\
 & m & \geq 1 \text{ and } \leq 2^m
\end{array}
$$
there are   nodes.

Levels $0,1,2,\cdots,(m-1)$ have the maximum complement of nodes, and level m has between one and 2^m nodes.

In a full tree, level m is full. Let the number of nodes in a full tree with maximum level number m be N_m. Counting the nodes at each level, there are

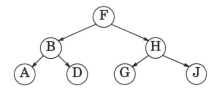

Figure 4.10: A Full Tree.

$$N_m = 2^0 + 2^1 + 2^2 + 2^3 + \cdots + 2^{m-1} + 2^m = 2^{m+1} - 1 \ .$$

Solving this expression for m in terms of N_m, the highest level number in the full tree can be written as

$$m = \log_2(\frac{N_m + 1}{2}) \ .$$

The number of levels in the tree is one more than the level number of the highest level, because the root is at level zero. In a tree with the minimum number of levels, the last level may be partially full. Thus, for a minimum level tree, the number n of nodes in the tree satisfies the inequality $N_{m-1} < n \leq N_m$. From the relationship developed above between N_m and m it is easily seen that $2^m - 1 < n \leq 2^{m+1} - 1$.

4.4.4.2. Full Tree Search Time

A full tree rarely occurs naturally in practice, although some algorithms that deal with trees will force a full tree to occur if possible. Nevertheless, it is clear that a full tree has the minimum number of levels of any tree having the same number of nodes. This fact makes the analysis of a full tree important. If all nodes are equally probable to be searched for, its result shows the best that can be done in searching a tree.

There are 2^j nodes at level j. Each node at level j needs $j+1$ node probes to locate it, because the levels are numbered from zero. The average time to search for a node is consequently

$$C_{N_m} = \frac{1}{N_m} \sum_{j=0}^{m} (j+1) 2^j$$

$$= \frac{1}{N_m} \left\{ \sum_{j=0}^{m} j\, 2^j + \sum_{j=0}^{m} 2^j \right\} \ .$$

After a mess of algebra (see details below), the result is found:

$$C_{N_m} = \frac{1}{2^{m+1} - 1} \left\{ m\, 2^{m+1} + 1 \right\}$$

$$= \frac{1}{N_m} \left\{ 1 + (N_m + 1) \log_2 \frac{N_m + 1}{2} \right\} \ .$$

As m gets large, $N_m \gg 1$, and

$$C_{N_m} \approx \log_2 \frac{N_m}{2} \quad .$$

In a full tree, the average time to search for a node is $O(\log N_m)$. This result is actually intuitive. There are 2^m nodes at the deepest level, and $2^m - 1$ at the lower levels. About half the searches will go to the deepest level.

The sum of the second series in the equation above is not difficult. It is is a geometric progression, so

$$S_2 = \sum_{j=0}^{m} 2^j = 2^{m+1} - 1 \quad .$$

The first series is a little more difficult.

$$S_1 = \sum_{j=0}^{m} j 2^j$$

$$= 0 + \sum_{j=1}^{m} j 2^j$$

$$= \sum_{j=0}^{m-1} (j+1) \, 2^{j+1}$$

$$= \sum_{j=0}^{m-1} 2^{j+1} + \sum_{j=0}^{m-1} j 2^{j+1}$$

$$= 2 \sum_{j=0}^{m-1} 2^j + 2 \sum_{j=0}^{m-1} j 2^j$$

$$= 2 \, (2^m - 1) + 2 \sum_{j=0}^{m} j 2^j - 2m \, 2^m$$

$$= 2 \, (2^m - 1) + 2 \, S_1 - 2m \, 2^m \quad .$$

Solving thjis equation for S_1 gives

$$S_1 = 2 \, ((m-1) \, 2^m + 1) \quad .$$

Actually, this series can be summed a little more easily by using a trick. Observe that $d \, a^j / da = j a^{j-1}$. The order of differentiation and summation can be reversed if the limits of the summation are independent of the differentiation. Using this, S_1 can be calculated as follows:

$$\sum_{j=0}^{m} j\, a^j = \sum_{j=0}^{m} a\, \frac{\mathrm{d}}{\mathrm{da}} a^j$$

$$= a\, \frac{\mathrm{d}}{\mathrm{da}} \sum_{j=0}^{m} a^j$$

$$= a\, \frac{\mathrm{d}}{\mathrm{da}} \frac{a^{m+1}-1}{a-1}$$

$$= a\, \frac{((a-1)m-1)a^m + 1}{(a-1)^2}$$

Letting $a = 2$ gives

$$\sum_{j=0}^{m} j\, 2^j = 2\,((m-1)\,2^m + 1) \quad .$$

Since $N_m = 2^{m+1}-1$, S_1 can be written in terms of N_m to give the desired result for C_{N_m} previously stated.

4.4.4.3. Arbitrary Tree Search Time

Suppose the tree has N nodes. An arbitrary tree at best will be a minimum level tree, and at worst will be a degenerate tree with a level for each node. A tree with as many levels as nodes is called a *vine*. The results for these cases are straightforward, and can be given in terms of the number of nodes probed. A node probe involves at least a comparison to determine which subtree to follow.

Worst Case:

The worst case happens when the tree is a vine, which is a form of a linear list. If a search for every node is equally probable, then the number of nodes probed is $N/2$ on average, half way down the vine.

Best Case:

A minimum level tree gives the best performance. The number of nodes probed on average is approximately $\log_2 (N + 1)$. This is actually the case when the tree is full.

For large N, the best case is much better than the worst case. If $N = 2047$, the worst case result is 1023.5 probes on average, while the best case involves 11 probes. However, for a tree built with data that is in arbitrary order, it is expected that the result will be closer to the best case than the worst case. Intuitively, there are a lot more trees having nearly minimum level than trees having one level per node.

In a successful search the information is in the tree and is actually found. In an unsuccessful search, the information is not in the tree and the search terminates at a null child. This indicates where the information can be inserted as a new node.

Let C_N be the number of nodes probed in a successful search of an N node tree, on average. Let C_N' be the number of nodes probed in an unsuccessful search of an N node tree, on average. We expect that the average number of nodes probed in a successful search, C_N, will be one plus the average number of nodes probed when that node was entered into the tree:

$$C_N = 1 + \frac{C_0' + C_1' + \cdots + C_{N-1}'}{N} . \tag{1}$$

The second term in this equation is the average number of nodes probed in building an $N-1$ node tree. The right hand side of the equation expresses the notion that C_N equals one plus the average number of nodes probed in building the $N-1$ node tree.

A *path* in the tree is an excursion from the tree root to some node in one of its subtrees. A *path length* is the number of links in a path. An *insertion point* is a link that does not lead to a tree node; it is one of the places that a new node could be attached to the tree. An *internal node* is any node in the tree not including any insertion points. The *external path length* E as the sum over all insertion points of the path lengths from a each insertion point in the tree, to the root. The *internal path length* I as the sum over all nodes of the path lengths from each internal node of the tree to the root.

Let k be some integer. In any tree, if we remove a node having no children attached to it, E decreases by $k+2$. Each external path to an insertion point will have a length $k+1$. After the node is removed, there will remain the single insertion point where the node previously attached, with path length k. Thus, $\Delta E = -(k+1) - (k+1) + k$. Also, after the node is removed, I decreases by k. The path to the removed node is deleted. As a result of removing the node, $\Delta(E - I) = 2$. Do this for each of the N nodes. Then

$$\sum_{i=1}^{N} \Delta(E - I) = 2N ,$$

but

$$\sum \Delta(E - I) = E - I ,$$

so

$$E - I = 2N \quad \text{so that} \quad E = I + 2N \ . \tag{2}$$

From the definition of I, it is evident that to conduct a series of successful searches finding each node once we must follow I links. Each path in each such search has one more node than its path length. So we must probe $I+N$ nodes. Hence the average number of nodes probed to find each internal node exactly once is

$$C_N = \frac{I+N}{N} \quad \text{giving} \quad I = N(C_N - 1) \ . \tag{3}$$

Any tree with N nodes will have $N+1$ insertion points in it. Thus, there are $N+1$ distinct unsuccessful searches. E is the sum of the path lengths to all insertion points. A search to an insertion point starts with the root, and has as many nodes in it as there are links in it. Hence the average number of nodes probed to find each insertion point exactly once is

$$C_N' = \frac{E}{N+1} \quad \text{giving} \quad E = (N+1)C_N'. \tag{4}$$

From Equations (2) (3) and (4),

$$E - I = (N + 1)\, C_N' - N\, (C_N - 1) = 2\,N \ ,$$

or

$$C_N = C_N' \, (1 + \frac{1}{N}) - 1 \ . \tag{5}$$

From Equations (5) and (1),

$$C_N' \, (1 + \frac{1}{N}) - 1 = 1 + (\frac{C_0' + C_1' + \cdots + C_{N-1}'}{N}) \ ,$$

or

$$C_N' \, (N + 1) = 2\,N + C_0' + C_1' + \cdots + C_{N-1}' \ . \tag{6}$$

This is a recurrence relation and is not hard to solve. We have Equation (6) and, with N replaced by $N-1$,

$$C_{N-1}' \, (N) = 2\, (N - 1) + C_0' + C_1' + \cdots + C_{N-2}' \ . \tag{7}$$

Subtract Equation (7) from Equation (6) to get

$$C_N' \, (N + 1) - C_{N-1}' \, (N) = 2 + C_{N-1}' \ ,$$

from which

$$C_N' = C_{N-1}' + \frac{2}{N+1} \quad .$$

For an empty tree the average number of nodes probed is zero, so $C_0' = 0$, and hence

$$C_1' = 1 \quad , \quad C_2' = \frac{5}{3} \quad , \quad C_3' = \frac{13}{6} \quad etc.$$

In general,

$$C_N' = \frac{2}{N+1} + \frac{2}{N} + \frac{2}{N-1} + \cdots + \frac{2}{3} + 1$$

$$= 2\,(\frac{1}{N+1} + \frac{1}{N} + \frac{1}{N-1} + \cdots + \frac{1}{3} + \frac{1}{2} + 1) - 2$$

$$= 2\,H_{N+1} - 2$$

where $H_{N+1} = \sum_{i=1}^{N+1} (\frac{1}{i})$, a harmonic progression. From Equation (5),

$$C_N = 2\,(1 + \frac{1}{N})\,H_{N+1} - 3\,\frac{-2}{N} \quad .$$

There is no crisp summation for the harmonic progression as there is for the geometric progression and for the the arithmetic progression. In order to get an approximate form for the value of the harmonic progression, the summation may be replaced with an integration, with the result

$$H_N = \sum_{i=1}^{N} \frac{1}{i} \approx \int_1^N \frac{1}{i}\,di = \log_e N \quad .$$

We have $\log_e N = \log_e 2 \times \log_2 N = 0.693\,\log_2 N$, and with the assumption that $N \gg 1$, C_N and C_N' are:

$$C_N \approx 2\,(1 + \frac{1}{N})\,\log_e(N+1) - 3 - \frac{2}{N} \approx 1.386\,\log_2 N - 3 \quad ,\text{and}$$

$$C_N' \approx 2\,\log_e(N+1) - 2 \approx 1.386\,\log_2 N - 2 \quad .$$

This is an important result. It shows that, on average, searching an arbitrary tree is about 39% more expensive than searching a full tree with the same number of nodes. We can conclude that the worst case, while very undesirable, is also quite improbable. In many cases, simple precautions suffice to make the worst case so improbable that we can forget about it actually happening in real situations. It is the case, however, that repeated additions and deletions of new nodes in the tree can evolve the structure of the tree into one that has vine-like proportions.

4.4.5. Binary Search Tree Node Deletion

When a node is to be deleted from a tree, the nodes that are its children must be reconnected to the deleted node's parent in such a way that the tree is still a binary search tree. In general, this is not easy. There are three cases:

Case 1: Deleting a leaf

This is easy. The leaf has no children. Free the space occupied by the leaf and remember to change the pointer that is a part of the parent of the leaf, and that previously pointed to the leaf, to equal nil(tree).

Case 2: Deleting a Node with One Child

This case is also easy. The node has exactly one parent (as do all binary search tree nodes) and exactly one child. Change the pointer in the node's parent that points to the node to be deleted to point to this node's child instead. The change of pointer disconnects the node to be removed from the tree. Remember to free the space previously occupied by the deleted node.

Case 3: Deleting a Node with Two Children

This case is more complicated. There are two children of the node that is to be deleted, and pointers cannot point to two things at once. The pointer in the parent of the node to be deleted, the pointer that used to point to the node that is now being deleted, can point to only one node after the deletion. When the node is removed there will be two subtrees to be reconnected. The strategy to overcome this problem involves bringing a node from one of the two subtrees to replace the node to be deleted.

Either of the two subtrees can be searched for a node that can be located at the spot in the tree that the deleted node previously occupied. Call this node the replacement node, and delete it from where it was found in the subtree. Instead, insert the replacement node in the tree at the spot where the node to be deleted was located. The two remaining subtrees, one of them intact and one of them modified after the deletion of the replacement node, are pointed to by the pointers in the replacement node.

Each subtree of the node to be deleted has one suitable replacement node. In the left subtree the suitable replacement node is the node that contains the largest data. It will have at most one child, so it can be easily deleted from the left subtree and become the replacement node. The node that contains the smallest data in what was the right subtree is the other suitable replacement node. It will also have at most one child, so it can be easily removed from the right subtree and become the replacement node.

Finding the replacement node is simple. For the largest data in what was the left subtree, start at its root and follow right links until a node with a nil right link is encountered. That is the node with the largest data in the left subtree, and it can be the replacement node. Notice that, by the way it is found, it will have at most one child. To find the smallest data in what was the right subtree, start at its root and follow left links until a node with a nil left link is encountered. Again, it will have at most one child.

Whether to go for the left replacement node or the right one is your choice. It can be affected by issues that are concerned with the evolution of the shape of the tree, such as those discussed in the next section.

All the above apparatus can be avoided if it is unusual to delete nodes. In that case, it is possibly sensible to include a *hereness* bit in the node. This bit can have two values, that are called *here* and *not_here*. If the *hereness* bit has the value *here*, the binary search tree operates exactly normally.

To delete the node, set the value of the *hereness* bit to *not_here*. The binary search algorithm is modified so that if the *hereness* bit is set to *not_here*, the search follows the left subtree if the usual comparison between the key and the data in the node indicates equality. Otherwise the search operates normally. The data will be physically in the tree, but it will be logically impossible to find it with the search algorithm.

Notice that if the data re-appears, it will be located at a different site in the tree. The tree will contain extra nodes, those that have been deleted by marking them *not_here*. If there aren't too many of them they should have an insignificant effect on the performance of the tree search. They can be properly deleted all at once in a restructuring of the tree such as that described in Section 4.4.7.

4.4.6. Balanced Binary Search Trees

There are two ways to prevent a tree from developing far more levels than it needs. In the first, the local structure of the tree at each node is continuously monitored, and the tree is incrementally rebuilt if some condition is violated. The other method involves a more *laissez faire* approach. The tree is allowed to grow without impediment. On an insertion it may be noticed that there are far more levels than there need be. When this happens, the tree is rebuilt to be a minimum height tree. Both methods have their good and bad points.

A binary search tree is said to be *balanced* if, at every node of the tree, the height of the left subtree differs by no more than one from the height of the right subtree. This definition describes just one kind of balanced tree. There are many others. This section will be concerned only with balanced binary search trees.

Each node has a right subtree and a left subtree. Let the height (in levels) of the right subtree at a node be h_r, and the height of the left subtree at the node be h_l. A property of each node of balanced tree is the *balance factor* of the node, defined as $b = h_r - h_l$. In a balanced tree $b = -1$, 0, or +1. The search of a balanced binary search tree proceeds as in any binary search tree. But insertion can lead to special cases. There are only two cases that cause trouble. The rest are reflections of the basic two.

The trouble that occurs on insertion is that the act of insertion can cause the balance factor at one or more nodes to exceed the allowed limits. In this case, the local structure of the tree must be altered to restore the balance factor to its proper range.

Figure 4.11 shows a tree that has become unbalanced because a new node has been added. The particular case is called an *outside* imbalance because of the part of the tree that has too many levels. The location of the imbalance can be far away from the site where the node is added.

To rebalance the outside imbalanced tree, an operation that is more easily pictured than described is to *rotate* it to reduce the imbalance. The standard search procedure still works properly, since we still have $\alpha < A < \beta < B < \gamma$ as before the balancing act. The tree of Figure 4.11, after rebalancing, changes to the tree shown in Figure 4.12.

If the new node that causes the imbalance is on the *inside* of the tree, an inside imbalance happens. This is shown in Figure 4.13.

The rebalancing involves a sequence of two rotations. The result of the first is shown in Figure 4.14, and the second gives the balanced tree shown in Figure 4.15. As before, the search still works because $\alpha < A < \beta < B < \gamma < C < \delta$.

The performance of a balanced tree can be deduced by analysis. The objective is to determine if the effort expended in keeping the tree balanced is worthwhile. The average height of the balanced tree can be used to obtain its performance. This result is known for full

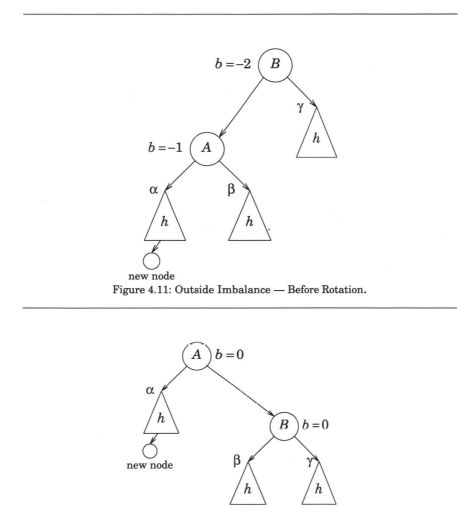

Figure 4.11: Outside Imbalance — Before Rotation.

Figure 4.12: Outside Imbalance — After Rotation.

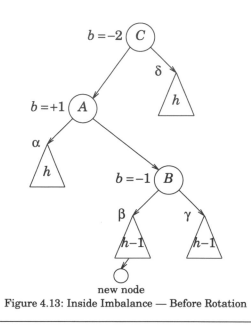

new node

Figure 4.13: Inside Imbalance — Before Rotation

trees ($\log_N$) and for arbitrary trees (1.39 $\log_N$). It is interesting to ask how balanced trees, particularly in the worst case, compare with these two situations. It will be shown that the height of a balanced tree with N internal nodes always lies between $\log_2 (N + 1)$ and 1.4404 $\log_2 (N + 1) - 0.3277$.

The first limit is easy. Suppose the tree has the minimum number of levels. Such a tree is obviously balanced. Then this minimum must be $h=\log_2 (N + 1)$. The quantity h is the number of levels, not the maximum level number m. Obviously, $h = m + 1$.

The search for the maximum height of a balanced tree proceeds as follows. A balanced tree of maximum height with h levels (to be found) containing N nodes is to be found. Clearly in such a tree the height of the left subtree of any node must be exactly one greater than the height of the right subtree of the node.

The search for this tree leads to Fibonnaci numbers. The quantity F_k is the kth Fibonacci number. $F_0 = 0, F_1 = 1$, and

$$F_k = 0, 1, 1, 2, 3, 5, 8, 13, 21, \cdots .$$

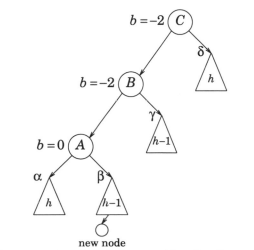
Figure 4.14: Inside Imbalance — After First Rotation.

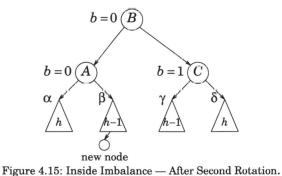
Figure 4.15: Inside Imbalance — After Second Rotation.

In this sequence, $F_{k+2} = F_{k+1} + F_k$ for k a non-negative integer.

A Fibonacci tree of order k, with a sequence of unique integers 1, 2, 3, $\cdots$ identifying each internal node, is the tree described by the following:

(1) If $k = 0$ or $k = 1$ the tree is empty.

(2) If $k \geq 2$, the root is the internal node designated F_k. The left subtree is the Fibonacci tree of order $k-1$. The right subtree is the Fibonacci tree of order $k-2$ with F_k added to all node identification numbers.

For example, Figure 4.16 is a drawing of a Fibonacci tree of order 5. The square nodes represent insertion points. They are not part of the tree, but are numbered for reference purposes from left to right. The circles are the internal nodes of the tree. The numbering of the insertion points has nothing to do with the numbering of the internal nodes of the tree. All the internal nodes of the tree are identified with the unique integer assigned by the method described above in (2) in the definition of a Fibonacci tree. Doing this will number the internal nodes in inorder sequence.

The same tree, without the detail but showing balance factors, appears in Figure 4.17.

It is apparent that the Fibonacci tree of order $h+1$ has the property that it has the fewest possible nodes among all possible balanced trees of height h. Any removal of a node will unbalance it.

It is easy but tedious to show that a Fibonacci tree of order k will have exactly $F_{k+1} - 1$ internal nodes. The Fibonacci trees of order 0 and 1 are empty. Evidently, the Fibonacci tree of order 2 has one node, with its left subtree being the empty order 1 tree, and with its right subtree being the empty order 0 tree. Also from inspection, the Fibonacci tree of order 3 has two nodes, with its left subtree being the one-node order 2 tree, and with its right subtree being the empty order 1 tree. Proceeding in this way, and using the recursive definition of the Fibonacci tree, the number of nodes in any Fibonacci tree of order k can be deduced to be $F_{k+1} - 1$.

A tree of h levels (we are trying to find h) is wanted. It must be a Fibonacci tree (so h will be as big as possible with the tree still balanced) with N nodes. Hence

$$N = F_{(h+1)+1} - 1 = F_{h+2} - 1.$$

If N is not exactly $F_{k+1}-1$ for some k, then

$$F_{h+3} - 1 > N \geq F_{h+2} - 1 .$$

A relationship between N and F_h has been developed. What is now needed is an expression for F_h in terms of h. It is known that $F_k = F_{k-1} + F_{k-2}$. Recurrence relations like $F_k = F_{k-1} + F_{k-2}$ often have general solutions of the form $F_k = A \, \rho_1^k + B \, \rho_2^k$. Substitute this into the recurrence relation to obtain

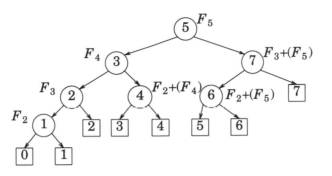

Figure 4.16: Fibonacci Tree of order 5: Construction Details.

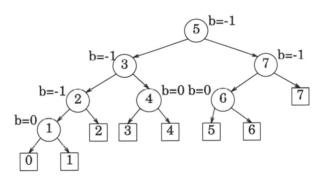

Figure 4.17: Fibonacci Tree: Balance Factors.

$$A \, \rho_1^k + B \, \rho_2^k = A \, \rho_1^{k-1} + B \, \rho_2^{k-1} + A \, \rho_1^{k-2} + B \, \rho_2^{k-2} \quad .$$

The quantities ρ_1 and ρ_2 are orthogonal, so separating this equation into two independent parts and dividing by the excess powers of ρ_1 or ρ_2 gives

$$\rho_1^2 - \rho_1 - 1 = 0 \quad , \text{and}$$

$$\rho_2^2 - \rho_2 - 1 = 0 \quad .$$

These have the solutions $\rho_1 = \frac{1}{2}(1 \pm \sqrt{5})$ and $\rho_2 = \frac{1}{2}(1 \pm \sqrt{5})$.

Let $\rho_1 = \frac{1}{2}(1 + \sqrt{5})$ and $\rho_2 = \frac{1}{2}(1 - \sqrt{5})$. These two constants are well known. The quantity ρ_1 is a constant called the *golden ratio* $\phi = \rho_1 = 1.61803....$ The related constant $\bar{\phi} = \rho_2 = 1 - \phi$.

The constants A and B are easily found. First, $F_0 = 0 = A + B$, so $B = -A$. Also, $F_1 = 1 = A \rho_1 + B \rho_2$. From these two equations, $A = 1/\sqrt{5}$. Finally, the solution of the recurrence is

$$F_k = \frac{1}{\sqrt{5}}(\rho_1^k - \rho_2^k) \ .$$

As k increases ρ_2^k approaches zero, so $F_k > 1/\sqrt{5} \ \rho_1^k$ for $k \gg 1$. But

$$N \geq F_{h+2} - 1$$

$$> \frac{1}{\sqrt{5}} \ \rho_1^{h+2} - 1 \ .$$

Solving this inequality for h in terms of N, and substituting for ρ_1, gives the desired result:

$$h < 1.4404 \log_2 (N + 1) - 0.3277 \ .$$

What has been shown is that at the expense of the balancing act, we can restrict the occurrences of expensive cases on search. Before, we had that the probable height for an arbitrary binary search tree was 39% more than the minimum height, and the worst height for the tree was N. For a balanced binary search tree the worst height is 44% more than the minimum height. The probable height is between this and the minimum. Balanced trees are of use only in the extremely rare circumstance where a very long search time would be a disaster, and the time spent rebalancing on insertion is tolerable.

4.4.7. Rebalancing Out-of-Balance Binary Trees

The previous section showed a way to store a binary search tree that was always balanced, in the sense that the height of any left subtree would differ by no more than one from the height of the corresponding right subtree. The tree balance had to be checked at every addition or deletion of a node. It involved keeping an up-to-date balance factor at each node, and checking it whenever a node was added or deleted. A more practical approach in many cases is to continue to use the tree until it gets seriously out of balance and then to rebalance it to have the minimum number of levels. The criterion of when this should be done will be dependent on the nature of the problem. Rebalancing could be triggered by search paths that are significantly

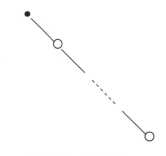

Figure 4.18: A Right-Only Vine.

longer than the minimum. It is easy to detect such paths as a side-effect of the search procedure.

It is important that the rebalancing act be efficient. The method that is presented here[1] has a complexity of $O(n)$, which is as good as can be expected. Consequently, a few extra rebalancings should not be a problem except in cases where the tree is very large. Extra rebalancing may also be due to frequent insertion and deletion activity.

The basic idea of the method is to convert the tree to a *right-only vine*. A *vine* is a tree in which each node (except the last one, the leaf) has only one child. A right-only vine is a vine that has another distinct property. In a right-only vine, every child is an only child and it is a right child. A right-only vine is shown in Figure 4.18. This tree-to-vine conversion can be done in $O(n)$ operations. Then the vine is converted into a tree with the minimum number of levels, again with $O(n)$ operations. The vine will have a sentinel node as its root, conceptually with an element that contains contents so tiny that all real elements will have larger contents. This is a reversal of the earlier convention that the root sentinel be huge. The sentinel root is used to make the algorithm simpler, so that it will have a right child only, like all other vine nodes with a child. Actually, in the programs the

---

[1]Quentin F. Stout and Bette L. Warren, *Tree Rebalancing in Optimal Time and Space*, CACM 29, September 1986, pp 902:908.

```
1   procedure rebalance( var root: pointer to tree)
    % This procedure rebalances the binary search tree
    % that has its root pointed to by the pointer "root",
    % with the result also pointed to by the pointer "root".
    % The treeToVine and vineToTree procedures are
    % used to do this.

2         var sentinelRoot: pointer to tree
3         var size: int

          % tree is declared as var tree: collection of node
          % and node is declared as
          %    type pervasive node
          %       record
          %          contents: typeOfElementsOfTheNode
          %          leftChildPointer: pointer to tree
          %          rightChildPointer: pointer to tree
          %
          %       end record
          % both declarations are elsewhere

          % get a root for the vine
4         new tree, sentinelRoot
5         tree(sentinelRoot).rightChildPointer := root

          % do the rebuild
6         treeToVine( sentinelRoot, size)
7         vineToTree( sentinelRoot, size)

          % reset the root of the real tree
8         root := tree( sentinelRoot).rightChildPointer
9         free tree, sentinelRoot

10  end rebalance
```

Figure 4.19: Tree Rebalancing — The Driving Program.

contents of the sentinel node are never assigned because no search down the vine is ever done.

For space efficiency, the vine is actually stored in the same collection as the tree. The program given in Figure 4.19 shows that sentinelRoot is the root of the vine, which is initialized in Line 5 to point to the same tree element as the root of the tree. This is the only new node required in the collection. Lines 6 and 7 call the procedures that do the work, Line 8 repoints the root at the (now balanced) tree, and Line 9 frees the node sentinelRoot.

```
1       procedure treeToVine( root: pointer to tree,
                              var size: int)
        % Transform the tree with sentinel root
        % pointed to by root into a vine with the
        % same root. Store the number of nodes
        % in the tree (and also in the vine) in size.
        % vineTail will point to the last node in the vine
2       var vineTail: pointer to tree
        % remainder will point to the rest of the tree
3       var remainder: pointer to tree
        % tempPointer is used in the rotation
4       var tempPointer: pointer to tree

        % Initialize
5       vineTail := root
6       remainder := tree(root).rightChildPointer
7       size = 0

8       loop
            % exit the loop when there is no remaining tree.
            exit when remainder = nil(tree)
            % head of the remaining tree have a left child?
9           if tree(remainder).leftChildPointer = nil(tree)
10          then
                % It does not. Shift VineTail down one node.
11              vineTail := remainder
12              remainder := tree(remainder).rightChildPointer
13              size += 1
14          else
                % It does. Do a rotation to shift a node to
                % the right subtree from the left subtree.
15              tempPointer := tree(remainder).leftChildPointer
16              tree(remainder).leftChildPointer :=
                            tree(tempPointer).rightChildPointer
17              tree(tempPointer).rightChildPointer := remainder
18              remainder := tempPointer
19              tree(vineTail).rightChildPointer := tempPointer
20          end if
21      end loop
22      end treeToVine
```

Figure 4.20: Tree Rebalancing — The Tree-to-Vine Program.

```
 1   procedure allRotRev( root: pointer to tree, count: int)
     % allRotRev works down the remaining vine nodes of the
     % tree pointed to by root, doing count rotations in reverse.

 2   var scanner, child: pointer to tree
     % scanner is a O vine node; child is a □ vine node
 3   scanner := root
 4   for i: 1..count
 5       child := tree(scanner).rightChildPointer
 6       tree(scanner).rightChildPointer :=
                               tree(child).rightChildPointer
 7       scanner := tree(scanner).rightChildPointer
 8       tree(child).rightChildPointer :=
                               tree(scanner).leftChildPointer
 9       tree(scanner).leftChildPointer := child
10   end for
11   end allRotRev

12   procedure vineToTree( root: pointer to tree, size: int)
     % Convert the vine with size nodes and sentinel root
     % pointed to by root into a minimum-level binary
     % search tree. The procedure uses the same rotation
     % that the treeToVine procedure uses, but in reverse.
     % The first time rotations-in-reverse are done
     % only enough are done to leave 2**(m-1) - 1 nodes down
     % extreme right child pointer path, and then
     % proceed as if size = 2**m - 1.

13   var leafCount: int              % number of nodes in the
                                     % maximum level
     var nodesLeft: int             % the remaining value of size

14   const LE2 := ln(2.0)            % log base e of 2
15   leafCount := nodesLeft + 1 - 2**(floor(ln(nodesLeft+1)/LE2))
16   allRotRev( root, leafCount)      % create max level nodes
17   nodesLeft := nodesLeft - leafCount
18   loop
19       exit when nodesLeft <= 1
20       allRotRev( root, nodesLeft div 2)
21       nodesLeft := nodesLeft div 2
22   end loop
23   end vineToTree
```

Figure 4.21: Tree Rebalancing — The Vine-to-Tree Program.

4.4.7.1. Tree to Vine

The tree-to-vine operation involves rearranging the pointers of the tree so they form a vine, with the sentinel root as the root of the vine. The rearrangement involves working down the tree node by node. An initial portion of the vine is created. A remaining portion of the initial tree will still exist. It will have nodes that all have contents larger than the contents of the nodes in the initial vine. At the start, the vine is empty and the remaining portion of the tree is the original out-of-balance tree. In the vine that is being constructed every node except the last has only a right child. The node nearest the root must have the smallest contents. The last node in the vine must have the largest contents.

In the tree-to-vine program shown in Figure 4.20, rotations exactly like those used in the balanced tree for the outside imbalance case are repeatedly done until the node at the head of the remaining tree does not have a left subtree. These are discussed in section 4.4.6. After the rotation, the contents of that node must be smaller than the contents of all the other nodes in the remaining tree, and it can be added to the end of the vine. Each rotation increases by one the number of nodes reachable from the sentinel root by only right links. No action ever decreases the number of nodes reachable from the sentinel root by only right links. Hence, at most $n-1$ rotations are done. The loop will be executed at most $2n-1$ times. This is because for each node down the vine, there will be at most $n-1$ rotations, and this will be done at worst for each of the n nodes. Hence the algorithm is $O(n)$.

4.4.7.2. Vine to Tree

The vine-to-tree program is shown in Figure 4.21. The algorithm is most easily explained for the case where $n=2^m-1$ for some integer m. In this case the final tree will be full, so there is not the annoying special case of the highest numbered level of the final minimum-height tree being partly populated. The more normal case when $2^{m-1}-1 < n < 2^m-1$ is easily handled and will be explained after the easy special case. The idea is to perform the balanced tree rotation shown in section 4.4.6 in reverse in a way such that the vine is gradually converted to a full tree.

Consider the sequence of steps that start with the vine shown at the upper right of Figure 4.22. Exclusive of the sentinel root, shown as •, there are seven nodes, and $7 = 2^3-1$. Alternate nodes of the vine are shown as □ and ○. In this case, after some rotations in reverse, the tree ends up full. The idea is to consider each group as shown in Figure 4.23 and to do the outside imbalance rotation in reverse, as shown. Performing the rotation-in-reverse for each such pair will produce the tree that is desired. The nodes remaining on the vine are said to be on the *spine* of the tree.

The procedure shown in Figure 4.23 repeats itself until there are as many nodes down the spine as rotations in reverse that have been done. Each of the nodes on the spine is alternately identified as either a □ or a ○ as was originally done, and the rotation-in-reverse process is repeated. The left subtrees that have been produced by previous steps get carried along with the subsequent rotations. This also happened in balanced trees, when during the rebalance the subtrees α and β got carried along. All of the left subtrees that get generated will be full, and the steps are repeated until a full tree is produced. At the end of the first step, there are 2^{m-1} nodes left remaining on the spine.

The vine has 2^m-1 nodes in it. After the first step, the spine has 2^{m-1} nodes. After the second step, the spine has $2^{m-2}+1$ nodes left. After the kth step, the spine will have $2^{m-k}-1+k$ nodes. A minimum height full tree with 2^m-1 nodes has m levels. When the spine has this many nodes, the tree will be full and the rotation-in-reverse steps can cease. Thus, the number of steps k that must be done can be determined from the equation $2^{m-k}-1+k = m$, and from this, $k = m-1$. When $m-1$ steps have been taken the final tree has been built.

Because of the way the algorithm operates, it should be evident that the leaves after the first step are the leaves of the full tree. This fact gives the clue about what to do when $n \neq 2^m-1$ for some m. When $n \neq 2^m-1$ for some m, let $\kappa = $ floor($log_2 n$). The first step is altered so that only $n-(2^\kappa-1)$ rotations in reverse are done. At the end of the first step the tree will have $2^\kappa-1$ spine nodes and $n-(2^\kappa-1)$ attached left subtrees. This will mean that some of the leaves in the full tree will not be populated, as expected. From the end of the first step the algorithm operates in the way it would have done had there been $2^{\kappa+1}-1$ nodes in the original tree.

The accompanying subprogram allRotRev does all of what has been called one step above. It is called first in Line 16 of procedure vineToTree to do the first step and then repeatedly in Line 20 to do the rest of the steps. The vine-to-tree procedure is O(n).

This algorithm for balancing a tree is efficient, simple, and elegant. To trigger its use, the tree algorithms should keep track of the number of tree nodes and the length of a search path. The tree can be rebalanced at the end of the search procedure if needed.

As mentioned in Section 4.4.5, the deletion of nodes from a tree is not nearly as straightforward as adding them to the tree. Whenever a rebalancing is done, nodes that have had the *hereness* bit set to *not_here* can easily be removed in the then clause of the treeToVine if statement.

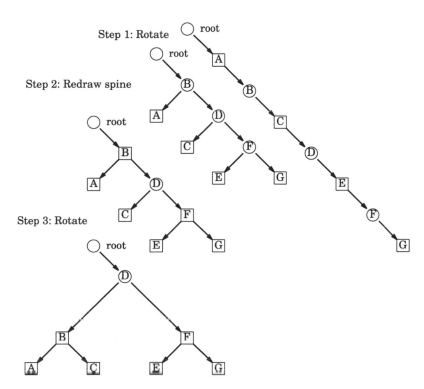

Figure 4.22: The Right-Only Vine to Tree Step.

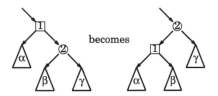

Figure 4.23: Tree Rebalancing — The Details of Each Step.

4.4.8. *j*-ary Search

It is interesting to investigate the case where there are more than two subtrees per node. The decrease in the number of levels might introduce a significant reduction in search time. The fairest comparison is likely to be the case when the trees are used as indexes to data objects. This is because in an index tree the search proceeds all the way to a leaf on all occasions, for all values of *j*. A tree used as an index has a pointer to a data object at each insertion point. It uses the tree structure only to choose which pointer corresponds to a given key. This is also the case most easily analysed.

Let there be λ data objects. Assume that the index trees have the minimum number of levels. Let the minimum height j-ary search tree that can index the λ objects have a maximum level number m_j. Then $m_j = \log_j \lambda / j$, and for a binary search tree, $m_2 = \log_2 \lambda / 2$. The ratio of maximum level numbers for a *j*-ary search tree and for a binary search tree is

$$\frac{m_j}{m_2} = \frac{\log_j \dfrac{\lambda}{j}}{\log_2 \dfrac{\lambda}{2}} = \frac{\log_j \lambda - 1}{\log_2 \lambda - 1} .$$

This ratio cannot exceed one.

Let η_j be the number of comparisons done per node to determine which subtree to search. Comparisons have a binary result. In a *j*-ary search tree, each node will need to contain $j-1$ items of information to determine which of the *j* links to subtrees should be followed. The information corresponding to link *j* will be equal to the largest information eventually pointed to by the subtree attached to link *j*. If simple brute force is used to determine which pointer to follow, the key is compared with the link information in ascending order. If the key is greater than the link *i* information, and less than or equal to the link $i+1$ information, link $i+1$ should be followed. Obvious special cases apply at the first and last link. On average, $(j-1)/2$ comparisons will be done by this brute force method. A much better approach is to use a binary search of the link information, so $\eta_j = \log_2 j$ comparisons are required at each node of the *j*-ary search tree. The analysis will assume that $\eta_j = \log_2 j$. As a special case $\eta_2 = 1$. In this case the link to follow is being determined as if there were a binary index tree with *j* insertion points and minimum height hidden in the node.

The number of comparisons used in a search is the number of comparisons required at each node times the number of levels in the tree. The ratio of the number of comparisons used in a *j*-ary search tree to the number used in a binary search tree is

$$R = \frac{\eta_j \, (m_j + 1)}{\eta_2(m_2 + 1)} = \frac{\log_2 j \, (\log_j \frac{\lambda}{j} + 1)}{\log_2 \frac{\lambda}{2} + 1} \quad .$$

This simplifies nicely when $j = 2^k$. Observe that $\log_2 2^k = k$. Let $\log_{2^k}(\lambda/2^k) = x$. Then $2^{k(x+1)} = \lambda$ and thus $x = (1/k) \log_2 \lambda - 1$. Hence

$$R = \frac{k \, (\frac{1}{k} \log_2 \lambda - 1 + 1)}{\log_2 \lambda - 1 + 1} = 1 \quad .$$

This is an astonishing result. In practice, of course, the number of links per node may not be exactly a power of two. This and the other approximations upon which the result is built may in particular cases mean that the ratio is a little less than one, so the j-ary trees are infinitesimally better. But the ratio will always be quite close to one. Therefore, if comparisons are a fair measure of performance, there is no advantage to the complications of j-ary search trees over binary search trees.

The entire process has assumed that the costly operation is the comparison. This is fair if the entire tree is in memory. In the case when the nodes are on disk, the cost of following a pointer is dominant. Then, it is evident that steps to reduce the tree height will be effective in improving performance because reading a node from disk will take on the order of milliseconds. This is on the order of more than three orders of magnitude slower that finding the next node in a tree stored in memory. The cost of deciding which of the j links to follow is insignificant compared to the cost of the disk read, and

$$R = \frac{m_j + 1}{m_2 + 1} = \frac{1}{k} \quad .$$

In this case the j-ary tree wins big.

4.5. EXERCISES

1. Suppose a queue is stored in an array. As insertions and deletions happen, the entries in the queue will move up the array. Design and program an algorithm that will properly let the contents of the queue wrap around the end of the array.

2. Suppose that the sequence 1, 2, 3, ..., n is permuted somehow into another sequence. Design and implement a program that will establish whether the new permutation of the sequence could have been generated with a stack.

3. Consider a queue and a stack in parallel. Input data can be entered in the queue (I) or pushed onto the stack (S). Output can be obtained from the queue (D) or the stack (X). What permutations can an admissible operation sequence achieve?

4. Consider two stacks in parallel. Input data can be pushed onto stack A (call this operation A) or stack B (B), and output can be popped off stack A (X) or stack B (Y). What permutations can an admissible sequence of A's, B's, X's, and Y's achieve?

5. Consider two stacks in parallel. Input data can be pushed onto stack A (A) or stack B (B), and output can be popped off stack A (X) or stack B (Y). In addition, the entry on the top of stack A can be pushed onto stack B (P), and the entry on the top of stack B can be pushed onto stack A (Q). What permutations can an admissible sequence of A's, B's, P's, Q's, X's and Y's achieve?

6. Suppose the data sequence 3, 1, 4, 1, 5, 9, 2, 6, 5, 3, 6 is inserted in a binary search tree in that order. Obviously, repeated values will not result in extra entries. Draw the resulting tree.

7. The integers 1, 2, 3, ..., 14 are inserted in a binary search tree in some unknown order. Suppose the tree has the maximum number of levels. Draw three such trees. Suppose the tree has the minimum number of levels. How many different minimum level trees are there?

8. Demonstrate by induction that a binary search tree with n nodes has $n+1$ places to insert a new element.

9. Do an inorder traversal, a preorder traversal, and a postorder traversal of the tree constructed in Exercise 6.

10. Obtain polish postfix expressions for the following four infix expressions.

   (1) $a_4x^4 + a_3x^3 + a_2x^2 + a_1x + a_0$.

   (2) $a_4x^4 + a_0 + x(a_3x^2 + a_2x^1 + a_1$.)

   (3) $x(x(x(xa_4 + a_3) + a_2) + a_1) + a_0$.

   (4) $a_0 + (a_1 + (a_2 + (a_3 + a_4x)x)x)x$.

   Place an ordering of expensiveness of computation on the four expressions. Assume that an expression requiring more stack depth is more expensive to compute than one needing less space in the stack.

11. How many levels would a tree with 1023 nodes have if it was minimum height? Maximum height? Average height?

12. Investigate the algorithm necessary to implement the balancing acts discussed in Section 4.4.6.

13. Suppose a sorted sequence of integers 1...n are to be inserted in a binary search tree. The rebalancing algorithm of Section 4.4.7 is to be used to minimize the search time. From an analysis of the situation, recommend a good criterion to use to trigger an invocation of the rebalancing algorithm.

14. Suppose a file of 14289238 records is kept on disk. An index tree is to be used to find any given entry. Each node in the index tree has up to j children. The computer memory available to hold an index tree node is limited to about a half-megabyte, reading a node from disk takes 40 milliseconds, and the computer can execute 10 million instructions per second. What value of j would you recommend?

15. Devise an algorithm to convert a tree with j subtrees per node to a binary search tree. One way to do this is by ordering the children of a node from left to right and then chaining them together with a series of links. The leftmost child becomes the only child (leftmost) of the original parent. If the original j-ary search tree was full, how many levels will the binary search tree have?

16. After doing Exercise 15, investigate the construction of a j-ary search tree rebalancing algorithm. The result of the algorithm should be a rebalanced j-ary search tree.

5 HASH TABLES AND HEAPS

5.1. INTRODUCTION

Recursive data types, mostly binary trees, were studied in the last chapter. A hash table is not a recursive data type. Only the second data structure — heaps — to be studied in this chapter is a recursive data type. Both data types are sufficiently different from those of Chapter 4 to merit their own chapter. Both data types are often overlooked. They both have features that make them extremely important in certain applications.

5.2. HASH TABLES

A *hash table* is a contiguous sequence of equal-size cells, searched with the aid of a *hash function*. Initially, each cell contains no data. A cell that has never held data is said to contain a blank. The information being searched for is called the *key*. To find the cell of a hash table corresponding to a key k, compute index $= h(k)$, where h is the hash function. The cell will contain a blank, or it will contain information corresponding to the key k, or it will contain information corresponding to some other key. When other information is encountered, a *collision* is said to have occurred. Various strategies can be pursued to resume the search when a collision occurs. These strategies distinguish different hash table techniques.

It should be obvious that the properties of $h(k)$ are important. Usually the number of elements in the domain of $h(k)$ is much larger than the number of elements in its range, so $h(k)$ is a many-to-one mapping.

5.2.1. Linear Hashing

In linear hashing, collisions are resolved simply by trying the next cell in a linear sequence. Suppose the table has M cells, indexed from 0 to $M-1$:

$$\text{index}_{j+1} = (\text{index}_j + \text{constant}) \bmod M \quad .$$

The mod function appears because index_{j+1} must lie within the table. The constant increment that determines any index from the previous one can be any integer. The resulting effects will be similar independent of the value used.

Example:

As an absurdly simple hash function, the mapping in Table 5.1 will be used. It would be a terrible hash function to use in practice, but it will serve to describe the technique. The key and the information are assumed to be one of the upper case letters.

Table 5.1: A Simple Hash Function.								
key	A P Q	B O R	C N S	D M T	E L U	F K V	G J W Z	H I X Y
$h(k)$	0	1	2	3	4	5	6	7

In this example, the hash table will have eight cells. The 26 letters each hash into one of the eight cells as shown in Table 5.1. The hash table is shown in Table 5.2, showing the changing contents of the eight cells that result from the stated operations. The constant increment is equal to the integer 1 in this table. The symbol b is used to denote a cell that once contained some information but is now empty as a result of that information being deleted from the table. It is necessary to remember that a cell once held data, because when searching, the information being sought might have previously been entered further down the table. It could have been inserted there when the cell now containing b contained some other information.

In general, scans of the hash table must continue until some cell that has never contained information is encountered. Only then is it sure that the information corresponding to the key is not in the table.

It is often convenient to think of a cell that has never been used as a *real blank*, and a cell containing b as a *pseudo blank*. During a scan, the location of the first pseudo blank that was found is remembered. If an insertion is required, this pseudo blank cell can be used.

Action	index	0	1	2	3	4	5	6	7	Probes
Load A	0	A								1
Load C	2	A		C						1
Load D	3	A		C	D					1
Load G	6	A		C	D			G		1
Load P	0	A	P	C	D			G		2
Load Q	0	A	P	C	D	Q		G		5
delete P	0	A	b	C	D	Q		G		2
delete Q	0	A	b	C	D	b		G		5
Load B	1	A	B	C	D	b		G		5
Load R	1	A	B	C	D	R		G		5
Load Q	0	A	B	C	D	R	Q	G		6

Table 5.2: An Sample Hash Table Showing Its Contents.

This will minimize the time of any later search for the object being inserted. In a subsequent search for it, the new information will be probed earlier in the search process.

The disadvantage of linear hashing is that the information tends to clump together. This results in an effect called *pileup*. Pileup is evident in Table 5.2. Pileup causes long searches, looking for a real blank, whenever an insertion is required. Other methods of collision resolution overcome this disadvantage by incrementing $index_j$ with something other than a constant to calculate $index_{j+1}$.

5.2.2. Choice of Hash Functions

Hash table methods depend in a fundamental way on the ability of the hash function to distribute the information evenly over the table, if good performance is desired. This should be true even in the case of two very similar keys, such as

LongStringOfCharactersA and
LongStringOfCharactersB.

Most hash functions treat the internal representation of the information as a number, regardless of what it actually means. They perform some numerical mapping process using this number as data. Most methods work well only if the table size, M, is a prime number. Otherwise, there is a strong possibility that an extended search will visit only a subset of all the cells, because the increment to compute a new index from the old one might be a factor of M. The best method is to use a *pseudo-random number generator*. This method uses the function $h(k) = (a \times k + b) \bmod M$.

The quantities a and b are constants. The values that should be used depend in a very direct way on the details of the way the computer does its arithmetic. Methods for selecting these constants have been studied in detail. It has been shown that b and M should be relatively prime, and that adequate performance is obtained if $a \approx M^{0.5}$, and that a should also be relatively prime to b and M. While there are no guarantees, this method can be very good and is the one most commonly used. Its properties are highly dependent on the values of the parameters a, b, and M.

5.2.3. Uniform Hashing

Uniform hashing overcomes the pileup problem inherent with linear hashing by incrementing $index_j$ with a quantity dependent on the key in a random way. Obviously, this increment can't be truly random, or it would be difficult to find any entry a second time. Define two hash functions

$$0 \le h_1(k) \le M - 1 \quad \text{and}$$

$$1 \le h_2(k) \le M - 1 \ .$$

For the reason mentioned above, M should be a prime number, so that neither h_1 nor h_2 divides it evenly. If M is prime, any choice of the $h_2(k)$ increment that is greater than zero will eventually cause the search procedure to visit all the entries in the hash table. Then

$$index_0 = h_1(k)$$

$$index_{j+1} = (index_j + h_2(k)) \bmod M$$

The hash functions are each evaluated once. Intuitively, the method will be better than linear hashing because the successive nodes probed are separated by a distance that is a function of the key.

5.2.3.1. Uniform Hashing Analysis

The analysis depends upon the assumptions that all keys are equally probable and that the hash functions are sufficiently good that all values in their range are equally probable. That is, that the hash function distributes the keys uniformly over the table.

There are M table locations, of which N are occupied, and $(M-N)$ are not occupied with a data item. The number of such combinations is $\binom{M}{N} = \dfrac{M!}{N! \ (M-N)!}$, all equally probable.

The probability P_r that exactly r probes are needed to insert the $(N+1)^{st}$ item is the number of the $\begin{bmatrix} M \\ N \end{bmatrix}$ combinations that has $(r-1)$ specific cells occupied (the $r-1$ collisions implied by the r probes), and another empty (the rth containing a real blank), divided by the total number of combinations $\begin{bmatrix} M \\ N \end{bmatrix}$. There are $(M-r)$ table locations other than the r that are committed, with $N-(r-1)$ of them occupied. Hence $(N-r+1)$ of these cells are committed, and the number of such arrangements is $\begin{bmatrix} M-r \\ N-r+1 \end{bmatrix}$, and

$$P_r = \frac{\begin{bmatrix} M-r \\ N-r+1 \end{bmatrix}}{\begin{bmatrix} M \\ N \end{bmatrix}} .$$

The average number of probes on insertion (an unsuccessful search) is

$$C_N' = \sum_{1 \le r \le M} r \, P_r .$$

This sum is messy, but it can be done. We will indicate how in the following subsection. The results, expressed in terms of the *load factor* $\alpha = \dfrac{N}{M}$ are

$$C_N' \approx \frac{1}{1-\alpha} ,$$

and the average number of probes on a successful search is

$$C_N = \frac{1}{\alpha} \ln \frac{1}{1-\alpha} .$$

As long as $\alpha < 0.8$ or so, implying that up to about 80% of the cells are occupied, the behaviour of a hash table is remarkably good. At $\alpha = 0.8$

$$C_N' = 5 \quad \text{and} \quad C_N = 2 .$$

It is significant that these results are independent of M. A successful search of a 99991 entry table (99991 is prime) with 79993 entries will, on average, take only two probes. An unsuccessful search will take only five probes. No other data structure is nearly as good from this point of view. A successful search of a typical binary tree with 79993 entries, assuming no obvious diabolical properties exist in the data, would take on average about 21 probes. An unsuccessful search of the same tree would take about 22 probes.

There are two important disadvantages of hash tables. First, it is difficult to deal with data that is not of fixed length. It is not always convenient to make the data of some fixed length. Second, the number M of cells in the table is fixed. There is no really satisfactory way to increase M dynamically without it becoming a big deal. Changing M means that the hash functions must change. The data already in the table will be hard to find with new hash functions. Consequently, every existing entry must be moved to a new location corresponding to the index calculated by the new hash function. It is awkward to distribute the existing data over the new table in a satisfactory fashion.

5.2.3.2. Details of the Analysis

It is desired to evaluate $C_N' = \sum\limits_{1 \le r \le M} r\, P_r$. The sum $\sum\limits_{1 \le r \le M} k\ P_r = k$ for constant k, because $\sum\limits_{1 \le r \le M} P_r = 1$. Hence

$$C_N' = \sum_{1 \le r \le M} rP_r = (M+1) - \sum_{1 \le r \le M} (M+1-r)\, P_r.$$

It is straightforward to do the necessary algebra to incorporate the $(M+1-r)$ factor in this equation into the combination $\begin{bmatrix} M-r \\ N-r+1 \end{bmatrix}$ that appears in the numerator of P_r. Doing this,

$$(M+1-r)\, P_r = (M+1-r) \frac{\begin{bmatrix} M-r \\ N-r+1 \end{bmatrix}}{\begin{bmatrix} M \\ N \end{bmatrix}}$$

$$= \frac{(M-r+1)}{\begin{bmatrix} M \\ N \end{bmatrix}} \frac{(M-r)!}{(M-N-1)!\,(N-r+1)!}$$

$$= \frac{(M-N)}{\begin{bmatrix} M \\ N \end{bmatrix}} \begin{bmatrix} M-r+1 \\ M-N \end{bmatrix} \ .$$

Hence

$$C_N' = (M+1) - \frac{(M-N)}{\begin{bmatrix} M \\ N \end{bmatrix}} \sum_{1 \le r \le M} \begin{bmatrix} M-r+1 \\ M-N \end{bmatrix} \ .$$

Let

$$S= \sum_{1 \leq r \leq M} \binom{M-r+1}{M-N} \quad .$$

Consider the table of binomial coefficients, commonly called Pascal's Triangle, shown below:

	B=0	B=1	B=2	B=3
A=0	$\binom{0}{0}$			
A=1	$\binom{1}{0}$	$\binom{1}{1}$		
A=2	$\binom{2}{0}$	$\binom{2}{1}$	$\binom{2}{2}$	
A=3	$\binom{3}{0}$	$\binom{3}{1}$	$\binom{3}{2}$	$\binom{3}{3}$

Each entry is of the form $\binom{A}{B}$, and it is well known that

$$\binom{A+1}{B} = \binom{A}{B} + \binom{A}{B-1} \quad .$$

This identity can be applied recursively to yield

$$\binom{A+1}{B} = \binom{A}{B} + \binom{A-1}{B-1} + \binom{A-2}{B-2} + \cdots \quad .$$

Since by definition $\binom{C}{D} = 0$ for D<0

$$\binom{A+1}{B} = \sum_{r=1}^{A} \binom{A-r+1}{B-r+1} = \sum_{r=1}^{A} \binom{A-r+1}{A-B} \quad .$$

Hence $S = \binom{M+1}{N} = \binom{M+1}{M-N+1}$, and

$$C'_N = (M+1) - (M-N) \frac{\binom{M+1}{M-N+1}}{\binom{M}{N}} \quad .$$

This simplifies to $C'_N = \dfrac{M+1}{M-N+1}$. Using the load factor $\alpha = \dfrac{N}{M}$ and the approximation $M \gg 1$,

$$C_N' = \frac{1 + \dfrac{1}{M}}{1 - \alpha + \dfrac{1}{M}} \approx \frac{1}{1 - \alpha} \ .$$

The results for a successful search are easily obtained from those for an unsuccessful search. We know

$$C_N = \frac{1}{N} \sum_{0 \leq k \leq N} C_k'$$

and

$$C_k' = \frac{M+1}{M-k+1} \ .$$

The harmonic series $H_n \approx \log_e n$ for large enough n, so the equation for C_N becomes

$$C_N = \frac{M+1}{N} \left[\frac{1}{M+1} + \frac{1}{M} + \frac{1}{M-1} + \cdots + \frac{1}{M-N+1} \right]$$

$$= \frac{M+1}{N} (H_{M+1} - H_{M-N})$$

$$= \frac{M+1}{N} \log_e \frac{M+1}{M-N}$$

$$= \frac{1}{\alpha} \log_e \frac{1}{1-\alpha} \ , \text{ where } M \gg 1 \ .$$

5.3. HEAPS

Consider the data structure shown in Figure 5.1a. Superficially it has the appearance of a binary tree, but it is not the sort of binary search tree that was studied in the last chapter. In this tree the data in every parent node is greater than the data in its children. This is obviously not a suitable layout for searching the tree for a given member. However, one consequence of this tree structure is that the largest node contents are in the root, and recursively the largest value in any subtree is at the root of the subtree.

The tree shown in Figure 5.1a is a minimum level tree, and all the elements in the last level are on the left side of the tree. Also, the

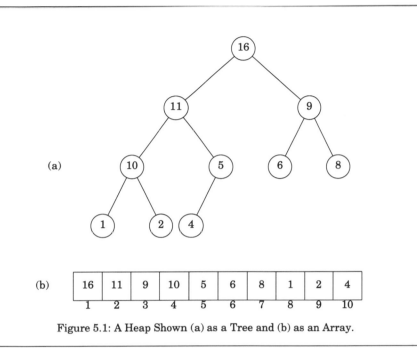

Figure 5.1: A Heap Shown (a) as a Tree and (b) as an Array.

contents of the nodes can all be stored in equal length fields. In this case they are all integers, which can be stored in one 32-bit word in most modern computers. This special situation has been contrived to allow the tree to be stored in a special way.

The array shown in Figure 5.1b stores the same data as the tree, but in a different and more compact way. The numbers beneath each element of the array are the index of that element. The children of element j, if they exist, are stored in elements $2j$ and $2j+1$. No space is wasted in the array by doing this. It is useful to distinguish between the children by calling the one at index $2j$ the left one, and the one at index $2j+1$ the right one. Compare the tree and the array to see how this works.

A tree of this type, stored as an array in the way shown in Figure 5.1b, is called a *heap*. It is very useful in applications that require the largest element of the data to be accessible quickly.

It will be shown that:

(1)   A new element can be added to the heap in $O(\log n)$ time;

(2)   If the largest element is removed, the remaining data elements in the heap can be rebuilt into a new heap in $O(\log n)$ time; and

(3)   An arbitrary array of n data elements can be built into a heap in $O(n \log n)$ time, using only a small number of temporary data storage locations.

5.3.1. Adding a New Element to the Heap

Suppose the new element 12 is to be added to the heap shown above. It is added to the end of the array as shown below. The resulting data structure is not yet a heap.

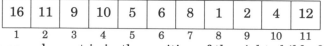

16	11	9	10	5	6	8	1	2	4	12
1	2	3	4	5	6	7	8	9	10	11

The new element is in the position of the right child of Element 5. A comparison of Elements 5 and 11 is done, and the larger placed in Element 5. A new Element 5 has been developed by this action. It is the right child of Element 2. The larger of Elements 2 and 5 is placed in Location 2. Finally, Elements 1 and 2 are compared. In the example, Element 1 is the largest element in the heap and no interchange need be done. The successive stages of the process are shown below, starting with the new array.

16	11	9	10	5	6	8	1	2	4	12
16	11	9	10	12	6	8	1	2	4	5
16	12	9	10	11	6	8	1	2	4	5

| 1 | 2 | 3 | 4 | 5 | 6 | 7 | 8 | 9 | 10| 11 |

The result is a heap. From an examination of the original tree structure, it is evident that a comparison of child and parent is being done at each level of the tree. The new element percolates up the tree until it finds a parent larger than it. There it stops. The tree is a minimum level tree with $n+1$ nodes. Such a tree has $O(\log n)$ levels, so in the worst case the algorithm runs in time $O(\log n)$. In the best case, the new element will not need to move, and the algorithm will take a constant time. In the average case, the algorithm runs in time $O(\log n)$, because the new element will need to percolate part way up

the tree. Since multiplying $O(\log n)$ by a constant will not change the
complexity, the average case is $O(\log n)$.

5.3.2. Rebuilding a Heap after a Deletion

Arbitrary nodes are not normally deleted from a heap. The only element that is deleted is that at the root. This is the largest element in
the data structure. After the largest element has been removed, the
heap will look like this:

11	9	10	5	6	8	1	2	4
1	2	3	4	5	6	7	8	9	10

A new heap can be built by moving the last element of the old
heap to the first position and allowing it to trickle down the tree,
swapping it with the larger of its two children as it goes, until both its
children are smaller than it. This process is illustrated below, beginning just after the largest element has been removed.

11	9	10	5	6	8	1	2	4
4	11	9	10	5	6	8	1	2	
11	4	9	10	5	6	8	1	2	
11	10	9	4	5	6	8	1	2	
1	2	3	4	5	6	7	8	9	10

```
Heapify: procedure(i,j)
        if i <= j div 2          % Are there any children?
            and [a child of aᵢ contains
                an element larger than aᵢ]
        then
            let aₖ be the largest child of aᵢ
            Interchange aᵢ and aₖ
            Heapify (k,j)
        end if
end Heapify
```

Figure 5.2: Heapify.

The 4 in the heap has trickled down to Location 4. The two children of the 4 in the heap, in Locations 8 and 9, are both less than 4. The 4 in the heap trickles no further. The procedure to rebuild the heap is shown in Figure 5.2. In this procedure the array is called a. The arguments i and j are the indexes in the array of the left and right ends of the heap. Heapify is called after a new element has been inserted at the root of an existing heap, in the example with Heapify(1,9) after the 4 is moved to the root.

```
Buildheap : proc
    for decreasing i: (n div 2)..1
        Heapify(i,n)
    end for end
```
Figure 5.3: Building the Original Heap.

5.3.3. Building the Original Heap

A heap can be built using the procedure Buildheap shown in Figure 5.3. Buildheap uses the procedure Heapify shown in Figure 5.2. It forms the heap by Heapifying the elements of a one by one, working from right to left.

1	2	3	4	5	6	7	8	9	10	
9	4	8	10	11	6	16	1	2	5	Original arrangement
9	4	8	10	11	6	16	1	2	5	after Heapify(5,10)
9	4	8	10	11	6	16	1	2	5	after Heapify(4,10)
9	4	16	10	11	6	8	1	2	5	after Heapify(3,10)
9	11	16	10	4	6	8	1	2	5	after Heapify(2,10)
9	11	16	10	5	6	8	1	2	4	after Heapify(5,10)
16	11	9	10	5	6	8	1	2	4	after Heapify(1,10)

Figure 5.4: A Heap Being Built.

The `for` loop in `Buildheap` starts with the last element of the array that has any children and `Heapify`s. It then does the second to last element, and so on, to the first element.

Suppose the original data were to be arranged as shown in Figure 5.4. The successive contents of the array will evolve in the way shown in the figure as the heap is built.

In the worst case (and the average case), each time i in `Buildheap` is changed, $O(\log n)$ comparisons of a parent and its children are done. The variable i is changed $O(n)$ times, so the overall complexity of `Buildheap` is $O(n \log n)$.

The procedure that was used to add an element to an existing heap could have been used to build the heap. Using `Heapify` is usually better (see the Exercises).

5.3.4. Williams' Heapsort

A Williams' heapsort is a sort that has the interesting property that it always is $O(n \log n)$, for any input data ordering. The data is arranged in a heap. It has been seen that this can be done with complexity $O(n \log n)$. In the following description, the data is assumed to be stored in an array a. The following array is a heap:

16	11	9	10	5	6	8	1	2	4
1	2	3	4	5	6	7	8	9	10

The central idea of the sort is building the heap.   `Buildheap` of the last section is one of the best ways to do this. Given that the original data has been put into a heap, it is not hard to see how to sort.

Element a_1 is the largest element of the heap. The sort proceeds by interchanging a_1 and a_n, thus putting the largest element in the correct location in the array. A heap with $n-1$ elements is then rebuilt using `Heapify`. For the example data above, the process proceeds as shown in Figure 5.5, where the sorted part of the data is shown in bold type.

The heapsort procedure is shown in Figure 5.6. This pseudo-program is easily rewritten in a real programming language. The only special requirement is that the language allow recursion. The requirement that `Heapify` be recursive can easily be circumvented because it is tail recursive. As usual, the non-recursive procedure lacks the elegance and clarity of the recursive version.

a_1	a_2	a_3	a_4	a_5	a_6	a_7	a_8	a_9	a_{10}
16	11	9	10	5	6	8	1	2	4
4	11	9	10	5	6	8	1	2	16
11	4	9	10	5	6	8	1	2	16
11	10	9	4	5	6	8	1	2	16
2	10	9	4	5	6	8	1	11	16
10	2	9	4	5	6	8	1	11	16
10	5	9	4	2	6	8	1	11	16
1	5	9	4	2	6	8	10	11	16
9	5	1	4	2	6	8	10	11	16
9	5	8	4	2	6	1	10	11	16
1	5	8	4	2	6	9	10	11	16
8	5	1	4	2	6	9	10	11	16
8	5	6	4	2	1	9	10	11	16
1	5	6	4	2	8	9	10	11	16
6	5	1	4	2	8	9	10	11	16
2	5	1	4	6	8	9	10	11	16
5	2	1	4	6	8	9	10	11	16
5	4	1	2	6	8	9	10	11	16
2	4	1	5	6	8	9	10	11	16
4	2	1	5	6	8	9	10	11	16
1	2	4	5	6	8	9	10	11	16
2	1	4	5	6	8	9	10	11	16
1	2	4	5	6	8	9	10	11	16
1	2	4	5	6	8	9	10	11	16

Figure 5.5: An Example of Williams' Heapsort.

```
Heapsort : proc
    Buildheap
    i := n
    loop
        interchange A_1 and A_i
        exit when i=2
        Heapify(1,i-1)
        i := i-1
    end loop end
```
Figure 5.6: Williams' Heapsort.

Heapsort is a two stage process. Buildheap is $O(n \log n)$. The main loop in the heapsort procedure is also $O(n \log n)$, because it does $n-2$ Heapifys, each $O(\log n)$. These two $O(n \log n)$ processes are done serially, so heapsort is $O(n \log n)$ overall. Furthermore, heapsort is always $O(n \log n)$. It is not particularly sensitive to the original data ordering. However, in practice the constant of proportionality is large, and usually quicksort is quicker than heapsort.

5.4. DISCRETE SIMULATORS

To a computer engineer, a *simulator* is a computer program that models reality and that usually has time as its independent variable. If time is being modelled as a continuous variable, or as a variable that changes in infinitesimal steps with monotonous regularity, the simulator is called a *continuous simulator*. In a *discrete simulator*, time jumps discontinuously from one *event* to the next. The time at which events will occur is forecast as a part of the simulation. A discrete simulator uses a mathematical model to determine that the next interesting event will occur at some future time and moves discontinuously to that time.

As an example of the use of a discrete simulator in electrical engineering, consider the simulation of a logic circuit. Discrete simulators are very useful in determining that a logic circuit behaves as predicted. Logic circuits are made up of devices that perform familiar functions, such as *and*, *or*, *nand*, *nor* and *not*, as well as memory cells. The relationship between the input variables to any such device and its outputs is well-known. When any input changes, it is known how the outputs will change. Each such output change will take some known time, often called the switching time or the gate delay of the device. In general, after the output changes, it becomes the input to some other device in the circuit.

Table 5.3: A Circuit.			
Inputs	Function	Outputs	Time Delay
I	Input	–	–
J	Input	–	–
I	not	K	5 ns.
J	not	L	5 ns.
I L	and	D	10 ns.
J K	and	C	10 ns.
D C	or	M	12 ns.

A simulation of a proposed circuit is often built before the circuit itself is actually constructed. It is very much cheaper and faster to build a simulator than to try to build the real thing from scratch. After the simulation demonstrates that the circuit should work correctly, the actual circuit can be built with some confidence that it will have few design errors, if any. Simulators are essential in the design of integrated circuits, because of the cost of building a new circuit and the time it takes to lay out the circuit on the substrate and to have it manufactured.

The circuit can be represented internally in tabular form in a way something like that used in Table 5.3. This example is far simpler than real circuits. Inputs I and J are complemented to give K and L, respectively. These four variables are then combined in a circuit that will give an output of 1 if and only if I and J are different. The overall function is called an *exclusive or*. It may be desired to simulate such a circuit to determine when the outputs change as a function of the inputs. The overall input-to-output functionality, as well as the timing, will be of interest. A block diagram of a simulator that can do this is shown in Figure 5.7.

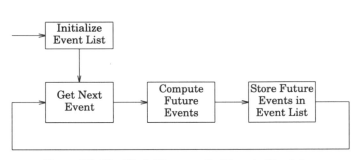

Figure 5.7: The Block Diagram of a Discrete Simulator.

The event list contains information about what variables in the circuit change and when they change. It is initialized with starting values for the input variables and, if they are known, with starting values for the internal variables as well. Future changes of the input variables are also put in the event list, including the time when they will happen.

The simulation starts with the extraction from the list of the events that occur at the next time of interest. The changes that these events cause can be predicted from the description of the circuit that is being simulated, and these are entered into the event list. The earliest events to occur are removed from the list, generating more events to be added to it, and so on. The simulation proceeds, alternately removing timely events from the list and adding future ones to it, until it encounters a special event in the list that instructs it to stop.

The event list could be sorted by time of event occurrence. In the simulation of a real circuit, there might be hundreds or thousands of events pending in the list, and keeping the list sorted could take rather a long time. In fact, however, the list need not be sorted, because the only events that are of immediate interest are those that occur next. A more sensible way to store the list is to make a heap, ordered by the times that future events will occur. Each entry in the heap contains its time of occurrence and a pointer to a list of the events that will occur at that time. The heap is arranged so that the root is the time of the next event. Figure 5.8 shows a sequence of events that might be put into a heap rather than a linear list.

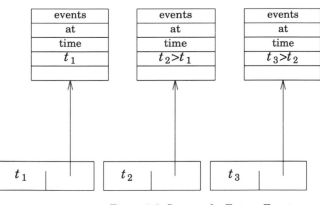

Figure 5.8: Storage for Future Events.

Getting the next event from the heap takes a small constant time. The next events are at the root of the heap and can be directly accessed. Future events can be added to the heap in a time $O(\log n)$ each, where n is the number of events in the heap.

If an array were to be used, the next event can still be found quickly. But inserting the future events in the array would take $O(n \log n)$ time, about n times more than it does with the heap. This is somewhat mitigated by the fact that the future events can be inserted in the array all at once, instead of one at a time.

5.5. EXERCISES

1. The example in Section 5.2.1 showed pileup in linear hashing. The different hash function shown below is to be used as the second hash function in uniform hashing.

Key	A	E	I	M	Q	U	X
	B	F	J	N	R	V	Y
	C	G	K	O	S	W	Z
	D	H	L	P	T		
$h_2(k)$	1	2	3	4	5	6	7

For the same sequence of actions that were done with linear hashing, investigate uniform hashing. Develop a measure to gauge which method is better, and compare them. Why is the result the way it is? Did you expect this sort of behaviour?

2. A hash table has 99991 locations, indexed with 0..99990. The function $h(k) = (317 \times k + 709) \bmod 99991$ is proposed as the hash function to find the first cell in the table to probe. The numbers 317, 709, and 99991 are prime, and 317 is approximately the square root of 99991. The quality of a hash function can be defined as the cardinality of the sequence $k_0, k_1, k_2, \cdots, k_n$, where $k_j = h(k_{j-1})$, for $k_0 = k_n$. Write a program that determines the quality of this hash function, for $k_0 = 10$ and $k_0 = 100$. Try other values of k_0 as well. Can you explain the result that you get?

3. An array contains the integers 3, 1, 4, 1, 5, 9, 2, 6, 5, 3, 6 in successive locations. Arrange these numbers into a heap, using the method of the procedure `Buildheap`.

4. In many circumstances, including a discrete simulator, it is required to add several new elements to a heap at the same time. Work out the best way to do this.

6 EXHAUSTIVE SEARCH

6.1. INTRODUCTION

To say an algorithm has *polynomial complexity* means that there exists a polynomial in powers of n that has a value that is always greater than the complexity of the algorithm. All of the examples of algorithms that have been presented so far have polynomial complexity. To see this, define $P_k(n)$ as a polynomial of order k. Then it is clear that $O(P_1(n)) = O(n)$, and $O(P_2(n)) = O(n^2)$. It is easy to see that $O(n \log n) < O(P_2(n))$.

Often when actual problems are solved with computers, the obvious algorithm is found to be more expensive than polynomial. It is not uncommon for exponential complexities, like $O(2^n)$, to crop up. When this happens, the time that is needed to compute some result may be far beyond that which would be considered reasonable or practical. There are three approaches that can be taken to handle such problems.

(1) Use a faster computer. Occasionally this tactic permits a problem that would otherwise be impractical to be solved. It is an expensive tactic, and in many cases the speedup is insufficient to make the use of an algorithm practical.

(2) Change the problem. Often algorithms with exponential complexity have special cases with complexity less than exponential. The resulting calculation may be practical if the original problem can be cast in terms of some special case. The problem is changed to be one of practical complexity, with a demonstration that a solution to this new problem can apply to the original case.

(3) Be clever about the problem. Many problems with exponential complexity can be approached in a way that does not formally make the complexity less. The extremely difficult cases will

still be impractical. But most cases will not be extremely difficult, and ways may (usually) be found to find an acceptable solution more quickly than the formal complexity of the problem implies. Instead of looking for an optimum solution to a problem, an intelligent search for *any* solution may yield an adequate result. It is not always necessary to persevere and find the optimum solution.

This chapter is concerned with the second and third alternatives. The first alternative boils down to solving difficult problems by pouring money on them and is not viable except in unusual circumstances.

The second alternative is often used. There is no way to generalize this tactic. The proper approach to take is too dependent on the idiosyncracies of the actual problem and on the precision needed for the answer. In several of the examples that appear later, special cases that are not as complex as the underlying algorithm will be identified where they occur. These particular cases do not necessarily arise in practice.

The third alternative is the one that can be studied in a general way, at least for some classes of problems. Techniques that guide the algorithm toward a likely solution will be examined. There will be no guarantee that there is an actual acceptable result in the direction that the solution is guided, but at least the most probable avenues of exploration will be inspected first. A class of algorithms known as exhaustive searches will be used as an example of exponential algorithms.

6.2. THE NATURE OF EXHAUSTIVE SEARCH

An *exhaustive search* explores the values that could be given to a set of variables to find an acceptable solution to some problem. Sometimes an optimum solution is required. This solution will satisfy some given criteria of optimality. A modification of the optimal solution problem is that the solution should satisfy some constraints, or have some sort of quality measure within known bounds. In other cases, any solution at all will do.

An exhaustive search will be used as an example of a problem with high complexity. It arises frequently in practice, and is amenable to study. As a generic example of exhaustive search, suppose that some problem has n independent Boolean variables to be determined. Each variable can have one of two values, true or false. Assume that the result of some known system of Boolean expressions is to satisfy a given quality measure. One such measure might be that the values of the Boolean variables are to be chosen such that the largest number of Boolean expressions are true. Since the variables are independent, there are 2^n different combinations of the values of the variables. Each combination must be tried for all the expressions. The problem is obviously $O(2^n)$ if each of these combinations must be inspected to see if it is the desired solution. Even if one half, or one thousandth, of the combinations must be inspected the problem is $O(2^n)$, because for constant k, $O(k\ 2^n) = O(2^n)$. Fortunately, in many cases the search for the desired combination can be guided such that, while the problem is $O(2^n)$, in practice a suitable solution can be found quickly. Tactics for designing such guidance are the essence of this chapter.

Exhaustive search is usually the basis of algorithms that play a game. In a game between two opponents, call each opportunity to move by each player a *ply*. Chess can be used as an example of a well known game. Programs that play chess are widely available. The best of them are reputed to play a very strong game but not quite as strong as the best human players. In chess there may be 20 or more legal moves at each ply. If 20 alternatives are to be examined at each ply, looking ahead seven plies (just four moves by the player doing the looking) means that $20^7 = 1280000000$ moves must be processed. If the computer is allowed six minutes per move, it must process a move in 93 nanoseconds. This is not long enough for any computer to generate the move and then to ponder what quality measure it should have.

The best human players sometimes look ahead far more than seven plies, because they have the ability through experience to reject whole sequences of moves as unproductive. This decision process is called *pruning*, and the best exhaustive search algorithms prune vigorously. All chess programs decide early in the search process that many of the moves that could be made at each ply are unlikely to have an acceptable outcome. These moves are ignored. The result is that sometimes sophisticated sacrifices that end up to be highly advantageous are not found. The sacrifices make the sequence of moves leading up to the desirable outcome have a quality measure so poor that the line of reasoning is abandoned. Human players often take the same approach and miss the advantageous outcome, too.

6.3. A SCENARIO FOR EXHAUSTIVE SEARCH

In a scenario for an exhaustive search, let there be n independent Boolean variables x_1 through x_n. Each variable can have a value of 0 or 1. In a real problem the range of values that a variable can assume

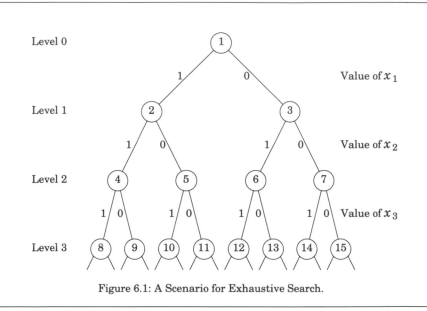

Figure 6.1: A Scenario for Exhaustive Search.

could be much larger. This exhaustive search scenario can be represented by a tree. The four levels nearest the root of the tree are shown in Figure 6.1.

The tree is an abstraction that is used to represent the reasoning followed by the algorithm. It describes the choices available to the decision-making procedure, but it has nothing to do with the actual problem.

In the figure, each link between nodes of the tree is associated with the assignment of a value to one of the variables. At level j there are 2^j nodes. Moving horizontally across the links between level j and level $j+1$, all the values that some variable can have appear 2^j times. Moving from level j to level $j+1$ implies that some tentative choice has been made for the value of a variable.

The exhaustive search algorithm proceeds by *expanding* node after node in the tree. Expanding a node means generating some or all of the children of the node. The first child to be expanded is called the *eldest* child. Also, this term is often used for the next child to be expanded in situations where some test is used to determine in what order to expand the children. Expanding the children of a node involves following some path in the tree, with the implication that some decision is being tried. Initially, no node is expanded. Part way through the search, some nodes may be fully expanded, some may be partly expanded, and some may have yet to be expanded. A fully expanded node is said to be *dead*, and a partly expanded node to be *live*. At the end of the search, all nodes will have been fully expanded — they will all be dead.

The algorithm starts with the expansion of the root node, numbered 1 in the tree above. There are four important and different tactics for the expansion process. They all fall into the general structure shown here:

```
 1   put the root node into a data structure.

 2   loop
 3       exit when the data structure is empty

 4       retrieve the next node from the data structure
               % call this node the present node

 5       if the present node is not dead then
 6           generate some new children of the present node
 7           do what is appropriate with a new child
 8           develop quality measures for the new children
 9           put the nodes in the data structure
10       end if

11   end loop
```

Statement 1 initializes a data structure with the root node. This data structure will contain all live nodes that have yet to be shown to have become dead.

In the loop, Statement 3 exits the search when all nodes are dead. Statement 4 retrieves from the data structure the next node to be expanded. This node is called the *present* node. The type of data structure determines which node is next. The type of data structure is one of the important distinctions between different exhaustive searches.

The then clause of the if statement also distinguishes between the various types of exhaustive search:

Generate some new children of the present node

Some types of search generate the eldest child of the present node that has yet to be generated. Others generate all the children of the present node at once. The generated child(ren) will be put into the data structure in Statement 9. The present node may be put back there too, if it is not dead.

Do whatever it is appropriate to do with a new child
> One of the things that is to be done is to check and see if a solution to the problem that is being searched has been found. Another is to see if there is any point in further exploration of this subtree and, if not, prune it. Bypassing Statement 9 will result in pruning the present node and all its children from the search.

Develop the quality measures for the new children
> The new children may have some sort of quality measure that can be developed. This quality measure is often an estimate of how far away the search is from a desirable solution to the problem. Some searches do not have a quality measure. They run automatically and blindly through all the nodes.

Put the nodes in the data structure
> The data structure will have some discipline for entering nodes into it. Push a node onto a stack, write it into the input end of a queue, and so on. The new children, and the present node if it is not dead, are put into the data structure. The order they are entered into the data structure can be determined by the value of the quality measure, if there is one.

The search tree that is being manipulated with this strategy is unlikely to be completely built. In most cases the tree is used to guide the search in a direction where some reasonably good answer can be found. Rarely in practice is the optimal answer actually needed.

6.4. DIFFERENT SEARCH TACTICS

There are many different search tactics that can be used but three of them are the most important ones. To give an example of each type of search, assume that there are only four levels in the tree shown in Figure 6.1. There are 15 nodes, as shown, numbered 1 through 15 for reference.

6.4.1. Depth First Search

A *depth first search* uses a stack as its data structure. In this search, the next node to be expanded is the eldest unexpanded child of the present node. A node that has been expanded is marked so that it will not be expanded a second time. The present node is pushed onto a stack when a new node is expanded. The new node becomes the present node. The nodes will be expanded in the order shown in the Figure 6.2. The figure also shows the implied decisions about the values of the variables that are made as the tree is searched.

A depth first search does an inorder traversal of the tree. It is called a depth first search because it quickly progresses as deeply as it can in the tree to find a tentative solution to the problem. There is little opportunity with a depth first search to adjust the order that the nodes are visited. It proceeds relentlessly and blindly as deeply as it can go. The only possibility of adjustment is the order in which the

Present Node	x_1	x_2	x_3	Remarks
1				Starting Point.
2	1			
4	1	1		
8	1	1	1	Is 111 a solution? Node 8 fully expanded.
9	1	1	0	Is 110 a solution? Node 9 fully expanded. Node 4 fully expanded.
5	1	0		
10	1	0	1	Is 101 a solution? Node 10 fully expanded.
11	1	0	0	Is 100 a solution? Node 11 fully expanded. Node 5 fully expanded. Node 2 fully expanded.
3	0			
6	0	1		
12	0	1	1	Is 011 a solution? Node 12 fully expanded.
13	0	1	0	Is 010 a solution? Node 13 fully expanded. Node 6 fully expanded.
7	0	0		
14	0	0	1	Is 001 a solution? Node 14 fully expanded.
15	0	0	0	Is 000 a solution? Node 15 fully expanded. Node 7 fully expanded. Node 3 fully expanded. Node 1 fully expanded. Finished.

Figure 6.2: Depth First Search.

children of a node are generated. If it is possible to test the children and to chose which is eldest, the best route down the tree may be tried.

It is easy to remember what node to return to after a subtree has been traversed. As with the inorder traversal, the present node is pushed onto a stack when the eldest child is generated. If the present node has no more children, it will be dead and the next node to be expanded will be the one on the top of the stack. If the present node has more children, the eldest of them is expanded.

It often becomes evident that there can be no solution down some branch of the tree. This could be due to some constraint being violated. If this happens, the present node can be abandoned, and the next present node selected from the stack top. An entire section of the tree has been pruned. No part of the section that has been pruned can be involved in the algorithm again.

A depth first search is obviously not suitable if the tree is not of finite depth. This can occur in problems that are formulated differently from the example given above. An example will be given later, in the discussion of the Game of 8.

6.4.2. Breadth First Search

A *breadth first search* uses a queue as its data structure. In a breadth first search, all the children of the present node are identified at the same time and saved in the queue. The nodes are entered in the queue eldest first. The eldest child is often equated with the one that has the largest quality measure. The tentative decisions for the values of the variables are stored in the queue with the node identifier. The node to be expanded next is the one that has been in the queue the longest. The present node has had all its children identified at the same time, so it is dead. It does not return to the data structure.

For the example started in the previous section, the nodes will be expanded in the order shown in Figure 6.3. The figure shows the queue contents as the search proceeds and the implied decisions about the values of the variables that are made as the tree is searched. The decisions are shown as subscripts to the queue entry.

Unlike the depth first search, a breadth first search searches the tree level by level. A quality measure can be developed for each child and they can be entered in the queue in order of highest quality. This ensures that when the search reaches this family of siblings, the one with the highest quality measure will be expanded first. It is not very likely that this tactic will make an important contribution to making the search more efficient. As with the depth first search, children for which a solution is not possible can be pruned.

The breadth first search is frequently used in cases where the tree is arbitrarily deep. Depth first search fails in this case, but breadth first search can succeed.

Present Node	Queue$_{x_1, x_2, x_3}$	Remarks
1_{--}	$2_{1--}\ 3_{0--}$	Starting Point. Node 1 Fully Expanded.
2_{1--}	$3_{0--}\ 4_{11-}\ 5_{10-}$	Node 2 Fully Expanded.
3_{0--}	$4_{11-}\ 5_{10-}\ 6_{01-}\ 7_{00-}$	Node 3 Fully Expanded.
4_{11-}	$5_{10-}\ 6_{01-}\ 7_{00-}\ 8_{111}\ 9_{110}$	Node 4 Fully Expanded.
5_{10-}	$6_{01-}\ 7_{00-}\ 8_{111}\ 9_{110}\ 10_{101}\ 11_{100}$	Node 5 Fully Expanded.
6_{01-}	$7_{00-}\ 8_{111}\ 9_{110}\ 10_{101}\ 11_{100}\ 12_{011}\ 13_{010}$	Node 6 Fully Expanded.
7_{11-}	$8_{111}\ 9_{110}\ 10_{101}\ 11_{100}\ 12_{011}\ 13_{010}\ 14_{001}\ 15_{000}$	Node 7 Fully Expanded.
8_{111}	$9_{110}\ 10_{101}\ 11_{100}\ 12_{011}\ 13_{010}\ 14_{001}\ 15_{000}$	Is 111 a solution? Node 8 Fully Expanded.
9_{110}	$10_{101}\ 11_{100}\ 12_{011}\ 13_{010}\ 14_{001}\ 15_{000}$	Is 110 a solution? Node 9 Fully Expanded.
10_{101}	$11_{100}\ 12_{011}\ 13_{010}\ 14_{001}\ 15_{000}$	Is 101 a solution? Node 10 Fully Expanded.
11_{100}	$12_{011}\ 13_{010}\ 14_{001}\ 15_{000}$	Is 100 a solution? Node 11 Fully Expanded.
12_{011}	$13_{010}\ 14_{001}\ 15_{000}$	Is 011 a solution? Node 12 Fully Expanded.
13_{010}	$14_{001}\ 15_{000}$	Is 010 a solution? Node 13 Fully Expanded.
14_{001}	15_{000}	Is 001 a solution? Node 14 Fully Expanded.
15_{000}		Is 000 a solution? Node 15 Fully Expanded. Finished.

Figure 6.3: Breadth First Search

Present Node	Queue $x_1 x_2 x_3$	Remarks
1_{--}	3_{0--} 2_{1--}	Starting Point. Node 1 Fully Expanded.
3_{0--}	7_{00-} 6_{01-} 2_{1--}	Node 3 Fully Expanded.
7_{00-}	15_{000} 14_{001} 6_{01-} 2_{1--}	Node 7 Fully Expanded.
15_{000}	14_{001} 6_{01-} 2_{1--}	Is 000 a solution? Node 15 Fully Expanded.
14_{001}	6_{01-} 2_{1--}	Is 001 a solution? Node 14 Fully Expanded.
6_{01-}	13_{010} 2_{1--} 12_{011}	Node 6 Fully Expanded.
13_{010}	2_{1--} 12_{011}	Is 010 a solution? Node 13 Fully Expanded.
2_{1--}	5_{10-} 12_{011} 4_{11-}	Node 2 Fully Expanded.
5_{10-}	11_{100} 10_{101} 12_{011} 4_{11-}	Node 5 Fully Expanded.
11_{100}	10_{101} 12_{011} 4_{11-}	Is 100 a solution? Node 11 Fully Expanded.
10_{101}	12_{011} 4_{11-}	Is 101 a solution? Node 10 Fully Expanded.
12_{011}	4_{11-}	Is 011 a solution? Node 12 Fully Expanded.
4_{11-}	9_{110} 8_{111}	Node 4 Fully Expanded.
9_{110}	8_{111}	Is 110 a solution? Node 9 Fully Expanded.
8_{111}		Is 111 a solution? Node 8 Fully Expanded. Finished.

Figure 6.4: Least Cost Search.

6.4.3. Least Cost Search

The two searches discussed so far differ in the data structure that is used to hold the nodes that are not yet fully expanded. A depth first search uses a stack, and a breadth first search uses a queue.

An obvious generalization of the above search techniques is to suppose that each child can have a quality measure evaluated for it when it is generated. The nodes can then be entered in a data structure so that they are ordered, with highest quality nodes first. The next node to be selected from the data structure will be the one with the highest quality measure. This is the basis for the *least cost search*, which is commonly used wherever a suitable cost function can be devised. Combined with pruning, it can be extremely effective at quickly identifying the most likely path through the tree to the desired solution.

This technique is quite powerful. In order to have an example of a least cost search, suppose that for unspecified reasons in the example of the last section it is preferred to have a solution with as many variables false as possible. Any other calculatable criterion would suffice. The list of nodes not yet fully expanded would be ordered by this criterion. Nodes associated with more variables with the value 1 will occur in the data structure after nodes with a smaller number of 1's. If the value of a variable is not yet known (represented as a - in the subscript), it could be a 0 and is ordered as a 0. Figure 6.4 summarizes the result of this technique.

The least cost search is effective in ordering the solutions that are tested by the number of 0's in the values of the variables. The tentative assignments to the variables are tested to see if they are a solution in least cost order.

6.5. AN EXAMPLE: THE GAME OF 8
In the late 19th century Sam Loyd patented a game he called the Game of 15. A square grid of 16 spaces has 15 tiles arranged in it, and one empty space. The tiles can be slid around, and the objective is to arrange them in the pattern

1	2	3	4
5	6	7	8
9	10	11	12
13	14	15	

from whatever starting configuration there was. A simpler version of the game, adequate for our purposes, has one row and one column deleted. There are now eight tiles in a grid of nine spaces. The resulting game is called the game of 8. The objective, called the *goal*, in the modified game is the following arrangement:

```
1 2 3
4 5 6
7 8
```

In order to refer to the arrangements of the tiles as they develop through the progress of a game, a number will be attached to the upper left corner of the board. The number will serve as a name for the particular arrangement shown in the board. It will also represent the order that the arrangements occur as the game progresses.

A cost of a particular arrangement will also be needed. In any exhaustive search it is useful if the calculation of the cost is as simple as it reasonably can be. The simple cost function that will be used is a count of the number of tiles that are out of position in the arrangement, plus a count of the number of moves that have been made away from the start of the game. This count will be reset to a previous value if we go back to continue the expansion of some previous node. The cost is appended to the lower right corner of the board.

For example, suppose that the arrangement shown below develops after the second move away from the starting arrangement.

```
8
  2   3
  1 4 6
  7 5 8
             7
```

This is the eighth board that has been developed in the game, so it is given the name 8. The cost of this arrangement is 7. The cost is obtained from 2 (moves from the start) + 5 (tiles out of place).

The moves will be described as *directions that the vacant tile moves*. Since any move must involve sliding a tile into the vacant space, the vacant tile seems to move. For consistency, the vacant tile will always be moved in the order RIGHT, LEFT, UP, DOWN, unless such a move is excluded for one of the following reasons: The vacant tile can not be moved off the board, and it is obviously futile to move the vacant tile back to where it was in the previous arrangement. Thus, there will often be less than four possible moves from any arrangement to the next. All the searches in the examples will start from the arrangement shown next:

```
1
  1 2 3
    4 6
  7 5 8
             3
```

6.5.1. Depth First Search

Depth first search does not use the cost function. Figure 6.5 shows the development of the arrangements. The eldest child of the starting arrangement involves moving the vacant tile to the RIGHT. Doing this gives the second configuration. Another move to the RIGHT gives the eldest child of the second arrangement. The eldest child of the third arrangement cannot be obtained by a move to the RIGHT (off the grid), or a move to the LEFT (move back to the second arrangement). The eldest child of the third arrangement, by the convention being used, will be a move UP by the vacant tile. It is not hard to see, as indicated by the figure, that this search will be indefinitely long, ending only if the goal arrangement is arrived at by a fluke. The seventh arrangement in the search has the vacant tile in the same place as it was at the start of the game. The other tiles have moved a bit, but not in a useful way.

While the depth first search is progressing as shown in the figure, the arrangements are pushed onto a stack. When there are no more children of some arrangement, the top element from the stack will be retrieved and the second eldest child expanded. In this example, this would never happen. Depth first search is a failure for this problem.

6.5.2. Breadth First Search

In contrast to ththe breadth first search finds the goal arrangement after examining 14 arrangements including the starting one. The progress of the game is shown in Figure 6.6. The children of a given arrangement are entered in the queue in the move order that is being used: RIGHT, LEFT, UP, DOWN. These are indicated in the figure by drawing them left to right. When the starting arrangement is

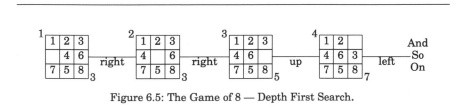

Figure 6.5: The Game of 8 — Depth First Search.

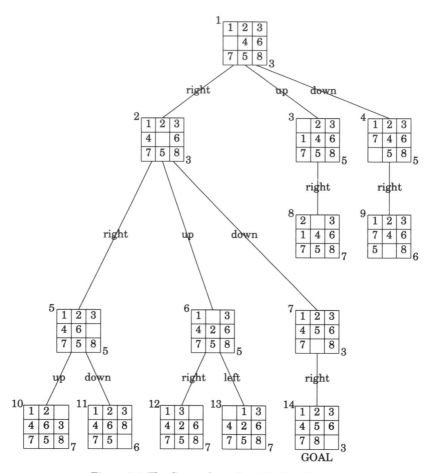

Figure 6.6: The Game of 8 — Breadth First Search.

expanded, the arrangements numbered 2, 3, and 4 are entered in the queue. The queue holds arrangements 2, 3, and 4 until the element at the head of the queue, 2, is expanded, its children are put in the queue, which then holds arrangements 3, 4, 5, 6, and 7. Again, the head of the queue is expanded, and the search proceeds as shown in the figure.

Arrangement 14 is the goal of the game, and the game stops there. An analysis of the moves that were made shows that the moves RIGHT, DOWN, RIGHT are a direct path to the goal. The breadth first search stumbles over this path in due course, by exhaustively examining all possible moves. Like the depth first search, the breadth first search does not use the cost to guide its search.

6.5.3. Least Cost Search
Examine the cost figures in the breadth first search. If the next node to be expanded is the one in the list with the least cost, the goal would have been found directly and rapidly.

It is convenient to adopt the convention of showing the cost of each node as a subscript of its node number. The children and their cost of the starting arrangement are
$$2_3, 3_5, 4_5.$$
This is what the list will hold after the starting node has been expanded.

The lowest cost node in the list is node 2. It is expanded, and the list contains
$$3_5, 4_5, 5_5, 6_5, 7_3.$$
These are sorted by cost to give the list contents as
$$7_3, 3_5, 4_5, 5_5, 6_5.$$
Node seven is expanded, immediately finding the goal. The search expands only nodes 1, 2, and 7 of the breadth first search. This is a great improvement.

Not all games are as effectively handled by the least cost search as the Game of 8. The problem usually is that the cost function is not as obvious or as effective as it is in the Game of 8. For instance, in chess the cost to be associated with a move is an unknown combination of dozens of factors, including things like board position, control of the centre, protection of own pieces, attacks on opposing pieces, the possibility of various ploys like forking two valuable pieces with a knight, etc. It is extremely difficult, perhaps impossible, to find a way to quantify all these elements of chess and to mould them together to develop the real cost of a move. The strength of a computer chess game is usually determined almost completely by such issues.

6.6. SATISFIABILITY
A Boolean variable can have only the values true and false. In this chapter, these values will be denoted by 1 and 0, respectively. The connectives and, or, and not are defined on Boolean variables in the

way that is expected from switching theory. The connective and will
be inferred from writing two variables in succession, so that x_1 and x_2
will be written $x_1 x_2$. The symbol + will be used to denote or, and not
x will be written $\bar{x}$. A Boolean formula is a combination of Boolean
variables and the connectives. If subscripted instances of x are the
Boolean variables, then $x_1 \bar{x}_2 x_3 + \bar{x}_1 \bar{x}_3$ is a Boolean formula:

A Boolean formula is said to be *satisfiable* if and only if it is true
for some assignment of values to the variables in it. Not all Boolean
formulas are satisfiable. Consider the formula

$$(x_1 + x_2 + x_3)(\overline{x_1 + \bar{x}_2 + \bar{x}_3})(x_1 + \bar{x}_2)(x_2 + \bar{x}_3)(x_3 + \bar{x}_1) \ .$$

If this formula is to be true, every one of the parenthesized terms
must be true. Consider the last three terms. If x_1 is true, then by the
last term x_3 must also be true if the equation is to be satisfied. If x_3
is true, then by the second last term x_2 must also be true. In fact, the
last three terms are such that if any of the variables has a value, then
the other two must have the same value if the formula is satisfiable.
Test this statement out. Set any variable to be true or false, and follow the reasoning above.

By the last three terms, if the formula is to be satisfiable all the
variables are true or they are all false. If they are all true, the second
term is false and the formula is unsatisfiable. If they are all false, the
first term is false and the formula is unsatisfiable. This formula is
not satisfiable. There is no combination of values that x_1, x_2, and x_3
can have that will result in the formula having the value true.

The formula shown above is sufficiently simple that we can reason about it. If a formula had hundreds of variables in about as many
terms, the problem would be impractical for human reasoning. For n
variables, an algorithm to test the formula would have to try all 2^n
combinations of values before it could decide that a given formula
definitely was not satisfiable. It might find a combination of values
early in the search that satisfy the formula, but before the algorithm
could assert with certainty that the formula was not satisfiable, all 2^n
sets of values would have to be tried, using any search.

Satisfiability is one of the famous problems of computer science.
A whole class of problems, called NP-complete problems, have been
shown to be equivalent to it. If any one of them could be solved by an
algorithm running in polynomial time, then they all could be solved in
polynomial time by suitably mapping one problem to another. So far,
nobody has been able to show that this is possible, or the more likely
case that it is impossible. It is certain that any such proof will not be
easy to find.

6.7. EXERCISES

1. In Section 6.3, the strategy for exhaustive searching was represented by a tree. What changes to the tree would there be if each variable could assume any values in the range 1..4? How would the complexity change?

2. In Section 6.3, the strategy for exhaustive searching was represented by a tree. Another type of strategy tree keeps track at each level of the values that have been assigned to all variables so far. From level 0 to level 1, the transitions are associated with values for x_1. From level 1 to level 2, the transitions are associated with values for x_1 and x_2. From level 2 to level 3, the transitions are associated with values for x_1, x_2, and x_3, and so on. Is this strategy tree a different shape? Why?

3. In the Game of 8, can all the starting arrangements that can be written down lead to a solution? Find a simple test to determine if some starting arrangement can be solved. (One such test might be based on observing what can be deduced when the starting game grid is scanned row-by-row).

4. Do a least cost search to solve the Game of 8, where the initial cost is 8 (every tile is in the wrong place). Make sure that there is a solution to your starting configuration (see Exercise 3).

5. The Boolean formula in Section 6.6 is called a 3-formula, because it has up to three literals per term. For a Boolean 2-formula there is a simple test to see if it is satisfiable.

    (a)   Find an unsatisfiable Boolean 2-formula.

    (b)   If your 2-formula uses a total of n Boolean literals, draw a figure in which each Boolean literal that is used is represented by a node and with the Boolean literals that are OR'ed together connected by a line.

    The figure you have drawn has a particular property that always exists for unsatisfiable Boolean 2-formulas, and never exists if the formula is satisfiable. What is the property, and why does it exist if and only if the formula is unsatisfiable?

7 PRINCIPLES OF PROGRAMMING LANGUAGES

7.1. INTRODUCTION

Users of programming languages have a tendency to fall into the trap of comparing them from the point of view of details of syntactic structure, or from a consideration of idiosyncratic features that happen to have been provided as part of the language. Whether or not a language includes an implementation of a generic data type to handle complex numbers, for instance, can be very important in the way that language can be applied to some problems but does not affect in a fundamental way the nature of the language. Languages like TURING and PASCAL, APL, and Fortran may differ in far more important ways than a compendium of sometimes useful features that may or may not have been implemented by the language designer or, often, by the compiler writer.

Programming languages fall into several classes, and members of one class do not differ much in principle from each other. These classes are distinguished by the following characteristics:

(1) There are several ways that the program can manage the memory that is allocated to it at execution time after it has been compiled.

(2) There are several ways that parameters can be passed to procedures and by which procedures can return results. Associated with these techniques are important properties called side effects that procedures may or may not have.

(3) The way a programmer indicates the type of data a variable is expected to contain can differ. The time at which this indication becomes effective, called the binding time, can also differ.

(4)   The span of source statements that can access a variable, called the scope of the variable, is different in different languages, and may vary while the program is executing, or may be fixed when the program is compiled.

(5)   A language may be designed to assist the programmer to determine if his program is correct, or it may leave that determination entirely to the good sense and intuition of the programmer and his ability to design and test his program.

All these attributes of languages just skim the surface of possible differences in languages. They apply in the most part to a class of languages called *procedural* languages, which constitutes the most successful group of languages designed so far. There is a great deal of research activity underway in the design of languages that have radically different principles than those commonly found in procedural languages. There are some languages, often directly or indirectly descended from the language LISP, that are worthy of study as potential competitors to the procedural languages, at least in some fields.

The thrust of this chapter is towards procedural languages. There is not room in this text to do justice to other classes of language, or to delve deeply into this subject.

7.2. MEMORY ALLOCATION

During *runtime* when a program is operating on its associated data, it requires enough memory to contain

(1)   the *runtime code*, which represents the sequence of statements that the programmer has written,

(2)   the *runtime package*, supplied from the library of programs associated with the language that is being used, which supports functions like input and output, the interface with the system software, and mathematical functions, and

(3)   the *runtime data* manipulated by the code. The programmer has declared most of this data.

The compiler produces the runtime code by translating a source program into an object program. The runtime code must occupy memory. There is little opportunity to be innovative in the way the runtime code is handled, because it must conform to the machine hardware and to the operating system software. However, there are different approaches that can be taken to the allocation of memory for the runtime data to occupy.

Static Runtime Memory Allocation

As the compiler is translating the source program, it can

Runtime Package	Runtime Code Space	Unused	Static Runtime Data Space

Figure 7.1: Static Runtime Memory Allocation.

determine how much memory each variable will occupy at runtime. The compiler can allocate space in runtime memory for this data in a static way, such that at runtime a reference to a given data element will always refer to the same memory location. This type of memory allocation is called *static* memory allocation, and it is found in many of the older procedural languages, particularly older Fortran compilers. A memory laid out in this way would be similar to that shown in Figure 7.1, which shows the memory space allocated to the runtime program, to the data, and a spare or unused part of memory.

Dynamic Runtime Memory Allocation

The compiler can allocate space in runtime memory for data in a more dynamic way, such that no specific memory location is identified by the compiler, but such that when each procedure (or the main program) is activated, a part of the runtime package without which no program can run, locates sufficient memory for the variables associated with that part of the program and assigns each variable to its proper part of that memory.

The runtime package uses a stack to hold the data it is dynamically allocating. When a new demand for memory occurs, because some new variables have become active, the runtime package allocates a block of memory on the top of the stack, and the individual variables are assigned their places within that block according to information provided by the compiler. When these variables are no longer needed, perhaps because of a return from a subprogram, the block can be popped off the stack. Both PASCAL and TURING use dynamic memory allocation. The layout of memory at runtime is shown in principle in Figure 7.2.

Runtime Package	Runtime Code Space	Unused	Stack Growth Area	Runtime Data Stack

Figure 7.2: Dynamic Runtime Memory Allocation.

Both these techniques have advantages and disadvantages. Static memory allocation avoids the invocation of the runtime package and so can be more efficient in most cases. However, the use of static memory allocation precludes recursion. Programs cannot be permitted to call themselves, directly or indirectly, because every invocation of a recursive procedure would use the same statically allocated memory location for the data that is pertinent to it, and the data from previous calls of the procedure would be overwritten.

With dynamic memory allocation, each new invocation of a procedure causes the allocation of a new block of data on the runtime stack, just for its own use. When it returns, this memory can be freed for further use by other procedures. In this way, the location in memory corresponding to a particular data variable may differ, because the contents of the stack may (and probably will) differ each time it is called.

7.3. PARAMETER PASSING

There are three different techniques of passing parameters to procedures. All appear in popular languages. Some languages use more than one technique, allowing the programmer to specify the technique to be used for each parameter passed.

The terminology that is used to talk about parameters is a bit confusing. When a procedure is called, it is *instantiated*. This means that an instance of it is created. A *formal parameter* is the parameter that is included in the declaration of the procedure. It formally represents a value of an *actual parameter* in the procedure. The actual parameter is the data value passed to the procedure as a parameter when it is called. The statement which caused the instantiation of the *called procedure* is located in the *calling procedure*. The actual parameters come from the calling procedure, and are passed to the new instance of the called procedure, where they are identified by names given to the formal parameters. For example, in the excerpt below the calling procedure is twink and the called procedure is foo. The procedure foo has formal parameters bug and rug, and is called with actual parameters 1 and gong in this sample of code.

```
procedure twink
      var gong: sometype
      procedure foo( bug: int, rug: sometype)
              % bug and rug are formal parameters
              % Whatever foo do comes here
      end foo
            .
            .
            .
      % call foo with actual parameters
      foo( 1, gong)
            .
            .
            .
   end twink
```

The three parameter passing techniques are:

Pass by Value

Pass by value passes to the subprogram the value of the actual parameter. The actual parameters are evaluated at the time the call is done. The formal parameter in the subprogram acquires this value. No result can be returned through a pass-by-value parameter.

Pass by Reference

Pass by reference passes to the subprogram a reference to the actual parameter. A reference is usually implemented by passing the address in memory of the parameter. The actual parameters are evaluated at the time the call is done. Any access to the formal parameter uses the reference to refer to the actual parameter. If the actual parameter is a variable name, the variable in the calling program will acquire a new value if the formal parameter is assigned a new value. If the actual parameter is a constant it must be "hidden" by passing a reference to a copy of the constant to avoid the possibility of the constant changing value. This has the same effect as passing the constant by value. If the actual parameter is an expression or hidden constant, its value can change, but this is not accessible to the calling program.

Pass by Name

Pass by name passes to the subprogram a reference to a small section of code (a *thunk*) which will evaluate the actual parameter in the environment of the calling program. The actual parameters are evaluated each time a formal parameter is accessed for a value. Any access to a formal parameter uses the reference to the corresponding thunk to compute the current value of the parameter. If the actual parameter is a variable name it will be passed by reference.

If the actual parameter is a constant it must be copied to a special location, with that location used as the parameter. This will avoid any changes to the value of the constant as seen by the calling program. It is meaningless to assign a value in the subprogram to a formal parameter that has had a reference to a thunk passed to it.

```
var x,y: int          % main program declarations
            .
            .
            .
procedure foo( a, b: int )
            var c: int          % a local variable
            c := a + b
            put c, a
            b := 3
            c := a + b
            put c, a
            return
end foo
            .
            .
            .
y := 5
x := 2
call foo( x × y, y )
call foo( y, 4 )
put x,y
            .
            .
            .
```

Figure 7.3: An Example of Parameter Passing.

A partial listing of a program is given in Figure 7.3. The program is written in no particular language, but its meaning should be clear. Assume it contains no errors. The code that is given includes the definition of the procedure *foo* and a small section of code that includes two calls to *foo* and the printing of some output values. A total of ten integers will be printed by this code. Table 7.1 shows the integers that are printed for the three methods of parameter passing.

Other than the obvious differences illustrated by this example, some more subtle differences exist between the three methods. Pass by value is elegant and clean. No vestige of the calling program can ever impinge upon the called program while it is executing. Call by reference can return results to the calling procedure through the parameter list, something that call by value cannot do. Such changes in the calling program caused by the execution of the called program are termed *side effects*. They are not necessarily bad, but can on occasion produce mystifying behaviour if they are not carefully controlled. Call by name can be terribly inefficient if the execution of the thunks takes extra time. For this reason, and because it is so prone to side effect difficulties, call by name is not used frequently.

With pass by value parameters, results must be returned in some way other than by changing the value of a formal parameter in the called program. On the other hand, pass by reference and pass by name parameters can return results to the calling program during the execution of the called program. In some languages, parameters identified as **var** will be passed by reference, and those not so identified will be passed by value. Sometimes functions are required to use pass by value parameters and are thus prevented from ever having side effects. On the other hand, a procedure must have a side effect if it is going to return a result, unless it deals only with output.

Passing an array by value is a tedious process, because a copy of it must be made. Many languages (for instance, PASCAL) always pass

Table 7.1: The Output of the Parameter Passing Example.										
by value	15	10	13	10	9	5	8	5	2	5
by reference	15	10	13	10	7	3	6	3	2	3
by name	15	10	9	6	7	3	6	3	2	3

arrays by reference, even though strict adherence to the principles of the language would require the array to be passed by value. There have been several attempts to design a runtime feature into languages that would permit an array to be passed by value but would prohibit any changes to it being visible to the calling procedure. So far, no such attempts have become generally used.

7.4. TYPING

Modern languages require that all variables be explicitly declared. This has not always been so. The early instances of Fortran implicitly declared all variables beginning with the letters I,J,K,L,M, and N to be integers (called FIXED in Fortran), and all other variable to be real (FLOAT). This resulted in common functions that happened to begin with the wrong kind of letter having their name changed, as in ALOG and IFIX. Many Fortran programs have been written without any explicit declarations appearing in them.

One of the reasons that modern languages have changed this is in order to introduce some redundancy into the program. The declaration of each variable can be checked by the compiler for type consistency with all uses of the variable. This has been found to be effective in the detection of errors by the compiler and has proven to be well worth the additional work on the part of the person who writes the code.

Languages that have no notion of declaration also exist. The type of a variable is the type of the last data object stored in that variable. APL is one such language. In APL, the type of the variable is bound to a data type at the last possible instant, as contrasted to the situation in TURING and PASCAL, in which the type is determined by the compiler from the declaration written by the programmer. It has been said that languages without types encourage programs that are difficult to read and understand and nearly impossible to demonstrate to be correct. These are sometimes referred to as *write-only* programs, implying that such a program can be written but never read.

7.5. SCOPE

At any point in a source program, a number of variables will be visible (that is, it is legitimate and non-erroneous to refer to them), while others may be inaccessible. The span of statements over which a variable is visible is called the *scope* of the variable. The rules that establish the scope of variables are the scope rules. The scope of a variable may change from point to point in a program. Often a change in scope implies that a different kind of access will be required to refer to the variable. There are three main types of scope:

Local Scope

Variables may have *local* scope, meaning that their declaration is local to the particular subprogram under consideration. If runtime memory allocation is dynamic, these variables will be in the top block of the runtime stack. If runtime memory allocation is static, all variables declared in a procedure are local to it by the n.ature of the way memory is handled.

Non-Local Scope

Variables with *non-local scope* are accessible within a given procedure but not declared within it. This occurs in PASCAL when a procedure declaration is contained within another procedure declaration. Variables of the containing procedure are accessible to, but non-local to, the contained procedure.

```
var x,y: int          % main program declarations
    .
    .
    .
procedure foo( a, b: int )
        var c: int            % a local variable
        a := 3
        c := a + b
        put c, a
        b := 3
        c := a + b
        put c, a
        return
end foo
    .
    .
    .
y := 4
x := 5
call foo( x × y, y mod x )
call foo( y**2+x, 4 )
put x,y
    .
    .
    .
```

Figure 7.4: The Code for Example 1.

Global Scope:

In most languages, it is possible to declare a variable to be of *global* scope. Such variables are visible everywhere. Global variables can be allocated statically in the same fashion that Fortran allocates all its variables, or dynamically in a special block at the base of the runtime stack. Variables that are declared at the outermost level of scope in most procedural languages are in effect global. Pervasive variables in TURING and variables in COMMON blocks in Fortran are global variables.

Some programming languages, for example TURING, do not have non-local variables because they prohibit nested procedures. The reason given for this concerns the efficiency of accesses to non-local variables. By their nature, they will be in some block of the runtime stack below the top block, and the provision of a mechanism called a *display* to establish their precise location at runtime is complicated. The management of a display is set up by the compiler such that regardless of the sequence of generation of new blocks on the runtime stack, all non-local variables can be located from the blocks that should be able to access them and are inaccessible from all other blocks. The compiler uses the scope rules to identify the blocks containing non-local variables.

The correct management of displays is complicated. It can result in considerable loss of efficiency. The language designers of

---

```
% declare some global variables
var Three, Four, BigDeal, Arcane: integer

% initialize some values
Three := 3; Four := 4
BigDeal := Three+Four

% declaration of an integer-valued function
Confusion: function(P,Q:integer):integer
        Q := P+Q
        result P+Q
end Confusion

% call Confusion to compute "Arcane"
Arcane := Confusion(Confusion(BigDeal,Three),Four)
```

Figure 7.5: The Code for Example 2.

TURING thought nested procedures a general capability that is of secondary usefulness. As the use of TURING spreads, perhaps the users will insist on this capability. Only time will tell.

7.6. EXERCISES

1. Work out what will be printed by the code in Figure 7.4, if the parameters are passed by value, by reference, and by name.
2. The code in Figure 7.5 is intended to use a special compiler, available only to us, that passes its parameters by name. The language is quite ordinary. Its statements mean the obvious thing. The compiler is known to operate properly. What value does the variable Arcane have after this code has been executed?

8 LANGUAGE DEFINITION AND STRUCTURE

8.1. INTRODUCTION

The principles used in the definition of programming languages are a very restricted subset of those used in natural languages. Many of the properties that are seen in programming languages arise from the necessity that a compiler must be able to translate a program in that language into a program in the language that is the instruction set of some machine. To be usable, the compiler must be quick and correct. The study of the principles behind the definition of programming languages will reveal many reasons why their general structure has evolved as it has.

8.2. LANGUAGES AND GRAMMARS

The permissible structures in a language are defined by a grammar. Languages and the basic notation used to describe them will be introduced first, followed by an introduction to grammars as they are used in compilers.

8.2.1. Languages

A set of *sentences* is made out of strings of *terminal* symbols. Let the set of terminal symbols be T. T is non-empty. If $a \in T$, then define $a^0 = \varepsilon$, where ε is the empty symbol, and $a^j = a\, a^{j-1}$, $j > 0$. For example, $a^0 = \varepsilon$, $a^1 = a$, $a^2 = aa$, $a^3 = aaa$, ...

Recall that the empty symbol is not the symbol that is normally called a blank or space. It is a void, a lack of any symbol, a nothing.

A string of symbols starting with α, then the empty symbol ε, followed by β, when written down as a single string will look like $\alpha\beta$. On the other hand, the empty set is a set that has no elements. It is *not* a set containing only the empty symbol. A set containing the empty symbol is not empty.

If X and Y are sets define $XY = [xy \mid x \in X, y \in Y]$. Define $T^0 = \varnothing$, where $\varnothing$ is the empty set, and $T^j = T\, T^{j-1}$, $j > 0$. For example, if $T = [a,b]$ then $T^0 = \varnothing$, $T^1 = [a,b]$, $T^2 = [aa, ab, ba, bb]$, and $T^3 = [aaa, aab, aba, abb, baa, bab, bba, bbb]$. Let $|T|$ denote the number of elements in the set T, and let $T^+ = \bigcup_{j=1}^{\infty} T^j$, and $T^* = T^0 \bigcup T^+$. T^+ is the set of all non-empty strings of symbols of any length that can be constructed from T. T^* is the set of all strings, including the empty string, constructible from T. The set of sentences in a language must be a subset of T^*.

8.2.2. Grammars

A grammar is a set of rules for choosing the members of T^* that are in a language and for excluding non-members. The rules of a grammar provide a means of testing if a sequence of symbols that might be a sentence really are one.

The obvious choice is a list of all members of the language. This can be expressed as $G = [\alpha \mid \alpha \in T^*]$, but in general $|T^*|$ is infinite, so in general the number of elements of G will be infinite. This makes it difficult to write G down. A method is wanted that will allow us to describe an infinite language (the number of sentences is infinite) with a finite, small set of rules.

A phrase structure grammar is such a method. A phrase structure grammar G is a collection $[N, T, P, Z]$ where N is a set of non-terminal symbols, T is a set of terminal symbols, P is a set of productions (see below), and Z is a special non-terminal called the goal.

It is required that $N \bigcap T = \varnothing$, so that we can distinguish non-terminals from terminals. This means that N and T can have no members in common. $N \bigcup T$ is called the *vocabulary*, V.

It is helpful if a consistent notation is used. The following notation will suffice. It isn't really necessary to make rules like this, of course, but it doesn't do any real harm.

greek letters denote $\in (N \bigcup T)^*$

> Any greek letter represents an arbitrarily long string of terminals and non-terminals. The empty string is included in the possibilities. There is no limit to the upper length of the string

represented by a greek letter. See the appendix for a list of greek letters and their names.

upper case roman letters like $A, B, C, D, \cdots$ denote $\in N$
An upper case roman letter chosen from the beginning of the alphabet represents a single non-terminal symbol.

lower case roman letters like $a, b, c, d, \cdots$ denote $\in T$
A lower case roman letter chosen from the beginning of the alphabet represents a single terminal symbol.

upper case roman letters like $\cdots, X, Y, Z$ denote $\in (N \cup T)$
An upper case roman letter chosen from the end of the alphabet represents a single symbol, either a terminal or a non-terminal.

lower case roman letters like $\cdots, u, v, w, x, y, z$
denote $\in T^*$ A lower case roman letter chosen from the end of the alphabet represents an arbitrarily long string of terminals. The empty string is included in the possibilities. There is no limit to the upper length of the string represented by one of these roman letters.

A set of productions P are re-writing rules of the form $\alpha \rightarrow \beta$, where α is a string in V^* containing at least one non-terminal and $\beta \in V^*$. There is at least one non-terminal in the left part of a production, while the right part can be any string in $(N \cup T)^*$. The production $\alpha \rightarrow \beta$ is read α *becomes* β.

Define the relation $\Rightarrow$, called *directly derives*, on strings in V^* as follows: If a string of symbols has a substring in it that is identical to the left part of a production, this substring may be rewritten and replaced by the right part. This rewriting action is why productions are also known as rewriting rules. If $\alpha \rightarrow \beta$, then the substring α in $\gamma \alpha \delta$ may be rewritten as β:

$$\gamma \alpha \delta \Rightarrow \gamma \beta \delta$$

The string $\gamma \alpha \delta$ is said to *directly derive* $\gamma \beta \delta$ with the production $\alpha \rightarrow \beta$. The relation directly derives relates two strings when the second is the result of applying a re-writing rule to the first.

Let $\xi_1, \xi_2, \xi_3, \cdots, \xi_n$ all be members of the vocabulary V^*. Suppose $\xi_1 \Rightarrow \xi_2, \xi_2 \Rightarrow \xi_3$, and so on with eventually $\xi_{n-1} \Rightarrow \xi_n$. This can be written as

$$\xi_1 \Rightarrow \xi_2 \Rightarrow \xi_3 \Rightarrow \cdots \Rightarrow \xi_n .$$

Then it is said that $\xi_1 \Rightarrow^* \xi_n$. The relation $\Rightarrow^*$, called *derives*, is the transitive completion of the relation $\Rightarrow$. Recall that a (binary) relation ρ on a set $S = [S_1, S_2, ...]$ is a set of pairs of elements in S. For any two elements S_i and S_j, the relation is said to be true if $[S_i, S_j]$ is in the set of pairs. Otherwise, the relation is false for these two elements. A transitive relation ρ is one such that, if $S_1 \rho S_2$ and $S_2 \rho S_3$

are true, then $S_1 \rho S_3$. If $S_1 \rho S_2$, ... , $S_{n-1} \rho S_n$ are true, then there exists a relation, usually written ρ^*, called the *transitive completion* of ρ, that is true for the pairs $[S_1, S_2]$, $[S_1, S_3]$, $[S_1, S_4]$, $[S_1, S_{n-2}]$, $[S_1, S_{n-1}]$, $[S_1, S_n]$, and the other pairs of members of S in the sequence of direct derivations ending with S_n.

The way that a grammar defines the language can now be stated.

$$L(G) = [\, w \mid w \in T^* \text{ and } Z \Rightarrow^* w \,]$$

In words, every sentence in the language L corresponding to a grammar G must be in T^* (must be a string of terminal symbols) and must be derivable from the goal.

Let $Z \Rightarrow \xi_1 \Rightarrow \xi_2 \Rightarrow \cdots \Rightarrow \xi_n \Rightarrow w$, where $w \in T^*$. Then $w \in L(G)$, and w is a sentence. The intermediate strings ξ_i are not sentences because they all contain at least one non-terminal. Each ξ_i is called a *sentential Form*.

Example 1:

$N = [Z, S]$, $T = [a, b, \ddagger]$, $P = [\, Z \to S\ddagger, S \to aSb, S \to ab \,]$.

What is L? Equivalently, what terminal strings can be derived from Z? Any sentential form that contains a Z can have the Z rewritten as $S\ddagger$. Any sentential form that contains an S can have the S rewritten as aSb, or as ab. Starting from the goal non-terminal Z, the language $L(G)$ can be derived and, in this simple case, written down. Usually the language is too complicated to be able to write it down.

$$
\begin{aligned}
Z & \\
& \Rightarrow S\ddagger \\
& \Rightarrow aSb\ddagger \\
& \Rightarrow aaSbb\ddagger \\
& \Rightarrow^* a^{n-2}Sb^{n-2}\ddagger \\
& \Rightarrow a^{n-1}Sb^{n-1}\ddagger \\
& \Rightarrow a^{n-1}abb^{n-1}\ddagger \\
& = a^n b^n\ddagger, \quad \text{for } n > 0,
\end{aligned}
$$

and hence $L(G) = [a^n b^n \ddagger \mid n \geq 1]$. The sentential forms are $a^{n-1}Sb^{n-1}\ddagger$ for $n \geq 1$.

Example 2:

$N = [Z, S]$, $T = [a, b, c, \ddagger]$, $P = [Z \to S\ddagger, S \to ab, S \to bc, S \to ca]$.

The derivations of all the sentences in this language are short:

Z	Z	Z
$\Rightarrow S \ddagger$	$\Rightarrow S \ddagger$	$\Rightarrow S \ddagger$
$\Rightarrow ab \ddagger$	$\Rightarrow bc \ddagger$	$\Rightarrow ca \ddagger$

$L(G) = [ab\ddagger, bc\ddagger, ca\ddagger]$, a finite language. Finite languages are not very interesting. In order for a language not to be finite, at least one of the productions must directly or indirectly define a non-terminal in terms of itself. For instance, a grammar containing the production $S \rightarrow aSb$ describes a language with an infinite number of sentences. The pair of productions $S \rightarrow aRb$ and $R \rightarrow Sc$ also imply an infinite language.

Example 3:
$$N = [Z, E, T, P], \quad T = [x, +, \times, (,), \ddagger],$$
and P is the productions

$$Z \rightarrow E\ddagger$$
$$E \rightarrow E+T$$
$$E \rightarrow T$$
$$T \rightarrow P\times T$$
$$T \rightarrow P$$
$$P \rightarrow x$$
$$P \rightarrow (E) \quad .$$

$L(G) = $ "well-formed" arithmetic expressions. This grammar is a classic. It is often known as "Everybody's Favourite Grammar" (EFG). It enforces the usual precedence rule for $\times$ over $+$ by collecting elementary objects into a P(rimary), then multiplying the Primaries together to form a T(erm), and finally adding the terms together to form an E(xpression). Notice that the language is infinite.

It is easy to add to Everybody's Favourite Grammar the other usual operators. Subtraction involves the production $E \rightarrow E-T$. Divide can be included with $T \rightarrow P/T$. Raise-to-power involves another layer of precedence. Remove the production $T \rightarrow P$, and replace it with $T \rightarrow F$ and $F \rightarrow P$. The introduction of the F(actor) in this way, along with the production $F \rightarrow F**P$ will do the job.

The negation operator is tricky to include. Probably the easiest way is to realize that an expression is permitted to begin with a minus sign only if the minus sign is the leftmost symbol in the whole overall expression, or if the minus sign is preceeded by a left parenthesis. Thus, add $P \rightarrow (-E)$ and $Z \rightarrow -E\ddagger$ as new productions.

The other operators, such as the relationals ($\geq$, $>$, $=$, etc.) and the Booleans (and, or, not, and perhaps others) are easily added with their normal precedence.

8.2.3. Types of Grammars

There are four types of grammars, depending upon restrictions on α and β in the production $\alpha \to \beta$. In practice, the only case of interest is if $|\alpha| = 1$. Since the left part of a production must have at least one non-terminal in it, $\alpha \in N$. The right part of the production $\beta \in V^*$, is any string of symbols in the vocabulary. This type of grammar is called a *context free grammar* (CFG) and defines a *context free language*. The string β is called a *phrase*, even if it is empty.

8.2.4. Recursion and Embedding

Consider the three grammars with the following productions. All three languages are expected to be infinite.

1:	2:	3:
$Z \to S\ddagger$	$Z \to S\ddagger$	$Z \to S\ddagger$
$S \to aaS$	$S \to aSa$	$S \to Saa$
$S \to a$	$S \to a$	$S \to a$

In each case $L = [a^{2n+1}\ddagger \mid n \geq 0]$. The derivations differ, however, in a fundamental and important way.

1:	2:	3:
Z	Z	Z
$\Rightarrow S \ddagger$	$\Rightarrow S \ddagger$	$\Rightarrow S \ddagger$
$\Rightarrow aaS \ddagger$	$\Rightarrow aSa \ddagger$	$\Rightarrow Saa \ddagger$
$\Rightarrow aaaaS \ddagger$	$\Rightarrow aaSaa \ddagger$	$\Rightarrow Saaaa \ddagger$
$\Rightarrow^* aaaa...a \ddagger$	$\Rightarrow^* aa...a...aa \ddagger$	$\Rightarrow^* a...aaaa \ddagger$

Right Recursion	Embedding	Left Recursion

The phrases at the bottom of the table above describe the nature of the derivation process that is happening. These terms are often used to refer to the kinds of productions that cause the type of derivations seen here.

Notice that in Everybody's Favourite Grammar both left recursion $(E \to E{+}T)$ and right recursion $(T \to P{\times}T)$ appear. Embedding also appears, but it is hidden by several steps. Combining the three productions $E \to T$, $T \to P$, and $P \to (E)$ gives $E \Rightarrow^* (E)$ amongst other things. This is, in effect, embedding.

Table 8.1: Canonical Deriving and Parsing.

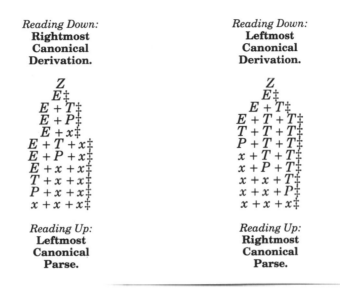

Reading Down:
Rightmost Canonical Derivation.

Reading Down:
Leftmost Canonical Derivation.

$$Z$$
$$E\ddagger$$
$$E + T\ddagger$$
$$E + P\ddagger$$
$$E + x\ddagger$$
$$E + T + x\ddagger$$
$$E + P + x\ddagger$$
$$E + x + x\ddagger$$
$$T + x + x\ddagger$$
$$P + x + x\ddagger$$
$$x + x + x\ddagger$$

$$Z$$
$$E\ddagger$$
$$E + T\ddagger$$
$$E + T + T\ddagger$$
$$T + T + T\ddagger$$
$$P + T + T\ddagger$$
$$x + T + T\ddagger$$
$$x + P + T\ddagger$$
$$x + x + T\ddagger$$
$$x + x + P\ddagger$$
$$x + x + x\ddagger$$

Reading Up:
Leftmost Canonical Parse.

Reading Up:
Rightmost Canonical Parse.

8.2.5. Canonical Parsing

Consider the derivations in Table 8.1, using Everybody's Favourite Grammar. The two different derivations, identified at the top of the table, have descriptive names. The *leftmost canonical derivation* always applies a rewriting rule (production) to the leftmost non-terminal in the sentential form. The *rightmost canonical derivation* always applies a rewriting rule (production) to the rightmost non-terminal in the sentential form.

The opposite of a derivation is a *parse*, and corresponding to each of the canonical derivations there is a canonical parse. Parsing is what compilers do when they are trying to recognize phrases and sentences in a programming language. After a few more preliminaries, parsing will be studied in detail.

A derivation can be represented in a tree-like structure, called a *derivation tree*, or more commonly a *parse tree*. The tree is the same for both derivations for an unambiguous grammar. The sentence is the tree's leaves. The parse tree for the accompanying derivations is shown as Figure 8.1.

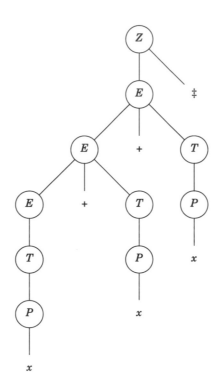

Figure 8.1: The Parse Tree.

8.2.6. Ambiguity

In the canonical derivations shown above, the order of application of the productions doesn't affect the terminal string derived. That is because the grammar is unambiguous. However, if the grammar is ambiguous, different derivations may have different parse trees. Consider the grammar with the productions

$$P = [Z \rightarrow E \ddagger, E \rightarrow E + E, E \rightarrow x]$$

The rightmost canonical derivation and the leftmost canonical derivation of the sentence $x + x + x \ddagger$ are both shown in Figure 8.2.

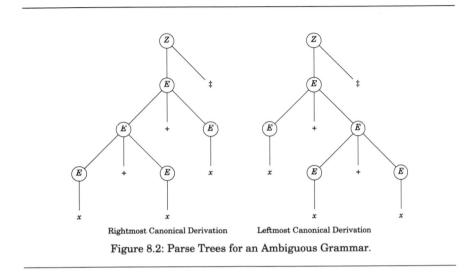

Rightmost Canonical Derivation   Leftmost Canonical Derivation

Figure 8.2: Parse Trees for an Ambiguous Grammar.

Depending on the order of application of the productions, the derivation tree is different. A grammar with this property is *Ambiguous*. Ambiguous grammars are nasty because the compiler has no way of knowing which of the derivations to prefer. The compiler must know exactly which derivation has happened if it going to be capable of sensibly interpreting the meaning (the *semantics*) of the phrases that its parser finds. In practice, ambiguous grammars must be avoided.

Some observations can be made about ambiguity:

(1)   Any grammar that contains a production that is both left- and right-recursive is ambiguous.

(2)   Suppose a grammar includes the two productions

$$c \rightarrow \textbf{if } b \textbf{ then } c \textbf{ else } c$$

$$c \rightarrow \textbf{if } b \textbf{ then } c$$

The following sentence is ambiguous:

$$\textbf{if } b_1 \textbf{ then if } b_2 \textbf{ then } c_1 \textbf{ else } c_2$$

The sentence can be parsed in two ways, as shown by the bracketing below:

$$[\textbf{if } b_1 \textbf{ then } [\textbf{if } b_2 \textbf{ then } c_1] \textbf{ else } c_2]$$
$$[\textbf{if } b_1 \textbf{ then } [\textbf{if } b_2 \textbf{ then } c_1 \textbf{ else } c_2]]$$

The obvious solution is to use some closing terminal token to match the **if**. For instance, if the grammar is changed as below, the ambiguity vanishes.

$$c \to \text{if } b \text{ then } c \text{ else } c \text{ end if}$$

$$c \to \text{if } b \text{ then } c \text{ end if}$$

Ambiguity is the a common problem when grammars are constructed. In some cases the cause can be quite subtle. The presence of ambiguity in a grammar implies that it is less than it should be, with probably difficulties appearing later when an attempt is made to use the grammar.

8.2.7. Constructing a Parser

There is a class of problems that are undecidable. For these, one can show that it is not possible to construct a general algorithm that will take any well-formed input and decide some question that has an answer that can be only true or false .

The problem of constructing an algorithm that will work for all well-formed input grammars to show whether a given context-free grammar is ambiguous, or if not, is undecidable. However, it can be decided that a grammar G is not ambiguous, or something is the matter with G. It may be ambiguous. This is all that is needed to conceive ways to construct parsers that correspond to unambiguous grammars.

8.3. EXERCISES

1. Let $S = [\,1, 2, 3, 4\,]$. List all the members of S^2.
2. Using Everybody's Favorite Grammar (section 8.2.2), write a rightmost canonical derivation of the sentence $x*(y + z*w)$.
3. Add productions to Everybody's Favorite Grammar to include (a) subscripted references to array elements, as in $A(i, j)$, (b) negation (unary minus), as in $-a$, (c) exponentiation (raise to power).
4. Work out a grammar for Boolean expressions. The operators *and*, *or*, and *not* are to be included. Add this grammar to Everybody's Favorite Grammar.
5. Develop a grammar for the language informally described as follows: All sentences are a string of a's and b's, with a single final ‡, Each a must be followed by at least two b's.

Table 8.2: Grammars for Exercise 10.			
Grammar	Productions	Grammar	Productions
G_1	$Z \to S\ddagger$ $S \to aFa$ $F \to Fb$ $F \to b$	G_2	$Z \to LJ\ddagger$ $L \to aF$ $F \to bF$ $F \to b$ $J \to ba$
G_3	$Z \to E\ddagger$ $E \to GF$ $F \to ba$ $F \to bF$ $G \to a$	G_4	$Z \to S\ddagger$ $S \to HJ$ $H \to K$ $H \to Hb$ $J \to bK$ $K \to a$

6. Develop a grammar for the language informally described as follows: All sentences are a string of a's and b's with a single c in the middle, followed by the single final $\ddagger$. Except for the $\ddagger$, every sentence is a palindrome.

7. Develop a grammar for the language informally described as follows: All sentences are a string of a's and b's and c's and d's, and a single final $\ddagger$. Except for the $\ddagger$, every sentence is a sequence of one or more substrings composed of a d followed by a palindrome of a's and b's with a central c.

8. Develop a grammar for the language informally described as follows: All sentences are a string of a's and b's and c's, with a single final $\ddagger$. A sentence is, from left to right, a non-empty string of a's, followed by a possibly empty mixture of a's and b's beginning with a b, followed by a c, followed by a possibly empty string of b's, followed by a possibly empty string of a's, followed by the final $\ddagger$.

9. From examining Everybody's Favorite Grammar, and the order in which it recognizes phrases, conclude for the usual arithmetic operators when it is preferable to use left recursive or right recursive productions.

10. The productions for four grammars are given in Table 8.2. Develop a succinct, symbolic expression for each of these languages.

11. The following are the productions for a grammar with goal Z that describes sentences in a language in which the terminal token operators O_1, O_2, and O_3 operate on the terminal token identifiers a, b, c, d, e, and f. For shortness, in the grammar the symbol ξ denotes exactly one of these terminal token identifiers.

$$Z \to A \ddagger$$

$$A \to A \ O_1 \ B$$

$$A \to B$$

$$B \to C \ O_2 \ B$$

$$B \to C$$

$$B \to O_3 \ C$$

$$C \to \xi$$

Parenthesize each of the following sentences to show the order that the phrases are identified in a left-canonical bottom-up parse. If you believe that any sentence contains an error, show the phrases recognized until the error is detected, and try to find a way to carry on parsing by either discarding the erroneous token, or by inserting another token in front of it.

$$a \ O_1 \ b \ O_1 \ d \ O_2 \ c \ \ddagger$$

$$c \ O_2 \ f \ O_2 \ e \ O_1 \ O_3 \ b \ \ddagger$$

$$e \ O_2 \ O_3 \ b \ O_1 \ c \ O_1 \ O_3 \ e \ \ddagger$$

9 PARSING AND COMPILING

9.1. INTRODUCTION

The obvious application of the material in the last chapter is in a compiler. This short chapter discusses the practical issues of parsing and gives an overview of the whole compiling process.

9.2. PARSING

The process of derivation is not too useful for the construction of a compiler. It starts with the goal and derives a string of terminal symbols. The opposite of derivation, starting with a string of terminal symbols and, by taking derivation steps in reverse (these are called parse steps), ending up at the goal, is called *parsing*. Parsing is exactly what a compiler needs to do. The following subsections describe some of the important notions and criteria associated with parsing.

9.2.1. Scanning and Lexical Analysis

It is normal to refer to the terminal symbols as *tokens*, since for convenience and efficiency successive related characters are combined together as the sentence is loaded into the queue, when this can be done unambiguously. For instance, a single token could represent each of the following:

$$=>, **, :=, \text{procedure, if, do,}$$

and so on. Additionally, comments, long strings of blank characters, and the like can be deleted or replaced with a single token. Even the names of the variables that the programmer has invented can be changed into tokens. The section of a compiler that makes these transformations is called the *scanner*. For reasons of efficiency, it is usually integrated with the procedure that reads in the source program. The scanner is itself a simplistic parser, looking for phrases like those listed above and transforming them as it passes them on. A parser-like program that transforms text in this way is called a *transducer*.

The lexical analyser is closely allied to the scanner. In a program, it is necessary to distinguish between variables that are declared locally in some procedure or other scope and those that are global or non-local. This is particularly true if two variables with the same name are declared in two different or nested scopes. When the scanner detects a variable name, the *lexical analyser* appends to this name information that will uniquely distinguish the part of the program that it was found in. It keeps track of the place in the program where the name occurred so that the correct correspondence between use and declaration can be made.

9.2.2. Types of Parsers

There are two major types of parsers. A *bottom-up parser* decides the specifics of a parse step by examining only the sentential form at hand. The various types of bottom-up parsers differ in principle only by having different algorithms that do the examination. All the important bottom-up parsers are known as shift-reduce parsers because of the way they operate. This will be discussed later.

A *top-down parser* examines the sentence or sentential form with a *read head* that moves (usually) left to right, starting at the extreme. It decides on the specifics of a parse step by, in effect, deciding which derivation from the goal ends with the sentence or sentential form identical to the one at hand, in the vicinity of the read head.

These two major subdivisions of parsers will be studied in subsequent sections.

9.2.3. Determinism

All parsers that are constructed should be *deterministic*, having at every stage a unique operation to perform. Situations where a choice must be made between several operations, and where there is no information available to make a choice, are called *non-deterministic* situations. A non-deterministic parser would have to guess at the alternatives repeatedly until it found the right one. This would require the parser to back up to a state it had previously been in, with the previous data restored, which might be possible but would be much too expensive, so that a compile would take a much longer time than it does now.

9.2.4. Error Recovery

For obvious reasons, parsers must behave sensibly for erroneous inputs. They must report each error they can find. Once an error has been found, the parser must recover so that it can continue the parse and find other possible errors. This recovery is not always easy. Error recovery techniques will not be studied further here.

Parsers that detect and report an error at the first opportunity are said to have the *error property*. Generally these parsers produce more sensible error messages and allow simpler recovery processes.

9.2.5. Speed and Space

Ideally, parsers are rapid and do not occupy a lot of space in memory. The ones that will be studied, when placed in actual use in a compiler, are sufficiently fast and small that they take about 10% of compiling time and less than 15% of the space used by the compiler. Further improvement is clearly beyond the point of diminishing returns.

9.2.6. Parser Generation

It is possible to write a parser by constructing an elaborate unit of complicated code, usually incorporating a combination of look-up tables and decision-making statements. Such programs are known as *ad hoc parsers*.

Algorithmic parsers use a formal algorithm to generate a parser from a grammar. This algorithm can be represented in a program, often called a *parser generator*. Some of the more sophisticated of this type of program are called *compiler compilers*. *Ad hoc* parsers are very occasionally of value, but they are harder to write, to document, and to debug, and they are nearly impossible to modify. Consequently, almost all modern parsers are produced by some sort of parser generator.

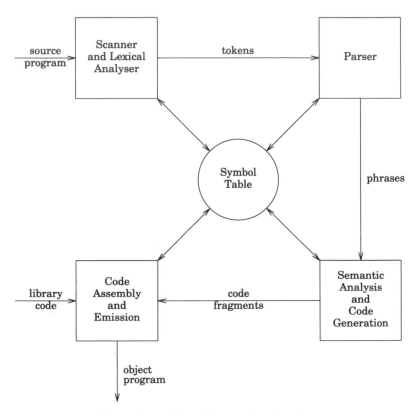

Figure 9.1: A Block Diagram of a Compiler.

9.2.7. Canonical Operation

A derivation or parse step will often have several possible alternative productions that could be used to rewrite one sentential form into another. It is known that if the grammar is not ambiguous, which rewriting rule is used is not important from the point of view of eventually deriving or parsing the desired sentence. However, a parser must decide which rule to use in some organized repeatable way. Otherwise subsequent processing in the compiler could become impossibly complicated.

Some rule for choosing which rewrite to do is obviously needed. A parser obeying the rule will be known as a *canonical parser*. The rewritings to choose are either the leftmost or the rightmost, because they can be found most easily. The leftmost is preferable, because the input tokens are usually available in left to right order. Parsers that make the choice this way are called *leftmost canonical parsers*. The sequence of sentential forms constructed by a leftmost canonical parser is exactly the same (in reverse order) as that constructed by a rightmost canonical derivation. This was described in Section 8.2.5. If the sequence of sentential forms in a rightmost canonical derivation are written on paper, with the goal at the top of the page and the sentence at the bottom, and then read from the bottom of the page toward the top, the steps of a leftmost canonical parse will be read.

9.3. COMPILERS

A compiler translates from a *source program* to an *object program*. The source program is written in a programming language. The object program is in some machine language so that, with the help of some services provided by the operating system, the object program is executable.

Compilers come in many different shapes and sizes. It is not really practical to describe a generic compiler, other than at a very high level of abstraction. Nevertheless, a simplified version of the structure of many compilers resembles that shown in Figure 9.1 reasonably accurately. This figure omits fundamental things like error recovery, the fact that most compilers make several passes through the source program, and the fact that most compilers re-order parts of the program in an attempt to optimize the code they produce. However, the principle of the way it works is evident.

The source code is scanned and lexically analysed. This may result in some entries being made in the symbol table. This table stores all information that is accumulated about variables, procedures, functions, and types. Tokens are passed on to the parser.

The parser discovers the structural properties of the program, statement by statement. It does a leftmost canonical parse. Some compilers will have the parser consult the symbol table, because it will discover some facts about variables as it progresses through the program. This will happen most often in variable declarations. The phrases that it recognizes are passed to the code generator.

The semantic analyser and code generator determine what calculation must be done to accomplish the semantics (meaning) of each syntactic phrase passed to it by the parser. It produces a fragment of code corresponding to this phrase in this context and passes it to the code assembler and emitter.

The code assembler and emitter assembles the code in the correct order, incorporates any library programs that are required, and finally processes it to reduce it to machine language. The machine language is the object program. It is written to a file for later loading into memory and execution.

There are a lot of different ways to do most of these steps. Probably the most sophisticated, and certainly the most interesting, is the parser. Several chapters of these notes are concerned with it. The next chapter will show in principle how an efficient, production quality parser can be constructed.

10 TWO REAL PARSERS

10.1. INTRODUCTION

This chapter presents two ways to build parsers. They are developed to a level where actual, practical, working parsers could be constructed. Needless to say, one of these two examples is a bottom-up technique and the other is a top-down one.

10.2. BOTTOM-UP SHIFT-REDUCE PARSERS

Figure 10.1 shows the general structure of all bottom up shift reduce parsers. They have three major parts.

The Queue

> The input text is perceived to be stored in a queue. The details of how it got there, and whether it is all there at once or appears in sections in some hidden way, are not significant to the basic operation of the parser. The output end of the queue (called its *head*) is the significant part. We assume that the next token of the sentence is available at the head of the queue. Some types of parsers will need to examine the first k tokens of the queue, starting at its head, in order to provide additional information for parsing decisions. In practice, in all such cases, $k = 1$ for performance reasons.
>
> It is important to realize that the objects in the queue will all be terminals. When it is desired to handle the object in the head of the queue, it is moved to a special data cell, called the on-deck circle. This is shown with the solid arrows in Figure 10.1. The non-terminal that is the result of doing a reduce (explained below) is moved into the on-deck circle as well.

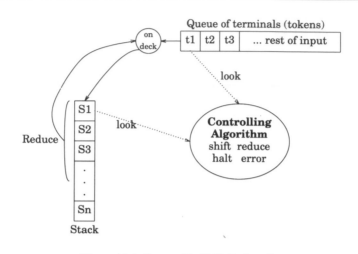

Figure 10.1: Bottom-Up Shift-Reduce Parsing.

The Stack

The stack is used as a storage structure for working data during the parsing process. The data that will be put in the stack can be thought of as members of the vocabulary (the terminals and non-terminals), but it is usual to put other data more associated with the parsing method in the stack. This is done for efficiency reasons.

In practice, each stack entry may well be quite elaborate. For instance, whether a terminal is a constant or the name of a variable may be irrelevant syntactically, but is vital semantically, and so this sort of information is usually included in the stack. Since the principles of the parsing process are not affected by this elaboration, we need only consider it peripherally.

The Controlling Algorithm

It is the controlling algorithm that distinguishes the types of bottom-up shift-reduce parsers. These parsers are classified by the type of controlling algorithm they use. The sections that follow describe one such parser that is based upon the controlling algorithm containing a Finite State Machine (FSM).

10.2.1. General Principles

Independent of the controlling algorithm, all bottom-up shift-reduce parsers operate according to similar principles. Initially, the input string is in the queue, the stack is empty, and the controlling algorithm is in a start state.

As parsing proceeds, the controlling algorithm does following:

- *Shift* a token from the input text (read it and remove it from the head of the queue) via the on-deck circle and push it (possibly along with related information) into the stack. Conceptually, the input text shifts one cell to the left in the queue.

- *Reduce* the tokens on the top of the stack. There will be a phrase in the top cells of the stack when this is done. They are popped off the stack, and a non-terminal is inserted into the on-deck circle. In effect, this applies a rewriting rule in reverse to the phrase of tokens on the stack top. The non-terminal that is inserted into the on-deck circle is chosen as the left-hand part of a production that has the phrase as its right-hand part. The non-terminal is put in the on-deck circle, and parsing resumes at the state corresponding to the data exposed in the stack top.

- *Detect an error* and call a special recovery procedure to deal with the error. This recovery procedure is responsible for reporting the error and for restarting the parser in a sensible way so any further errors can be found. Recovery procedures have few options. They can discard an input token or insert a plausible new token in front of the queue. It is something of an art to produce understandable error messages. Whatever the recovery action, it must eventually lead to exhaustion of the input text, even if parsing never gets properly started again. Otherwise, the parser might loop with some specific errors.

$$0: Z \rightarrow S\ddagger$$
$$1: S \rightarrow aSb$$
$$2: S \rightarrow ab$$

$$L(G) = [\ a^n\ b^n\ \ddagger\ |\ n \geq 1].$$

Figure 10.2: A Grammar for the FSM Example.

- *Halt* successfully. The queue will be empty. The stack will contain the goal non-terminal.

All through the parsing process, the sentential form currently being manipulated exists in the stack and queue. Reading tokens from the bottom of the stack toward its top, and then reading across the queue, reveals the sentential form.

10.2.2. FSM Parsers

One of the most important types of bottom-up shift-reduce parsers is controlled by a Finite State Machine (FSM). This is an abstract machine having states and transitions between states. Two special states are the start state and the halt state. The operation of such a parser will be described by way of an example.

10.2.2.1. An FSM Example:

The productions of an example grammar are given in Figure 10.2. The language is also given. It is an extremely simple case, but it will suffice for the purpose of becoming acquainted with the technique.

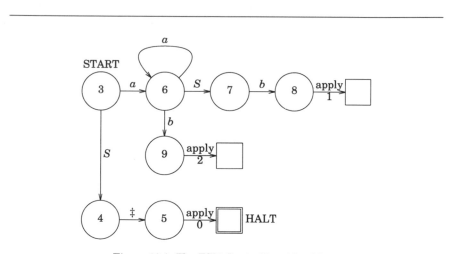

Figure 10.3: The FSM Controlling Algorithm.

Later on a much more elaborate example will be given.

10.2.2.2. The Controlling Algorithm

The finite state machine in Figure 10.3 is the controlling algorithm
for the grammar of Figure 10.2. It is composed of shift states, reduce
states, and transitions. The productions are each given a number.
Conventionally, the goal production is production 0, but this is not
necessary for the method to work.

Shift States

The shift states (circles) are entered with transitions from other
shift states. They are numbered beginning at the start state.
The start state is given the number of the lowest integer greater
than that of the highest numbered production. This keeps the
state numbers distinct from the numbers of the productions. In
Figure 10.3, the productions use the integers 0, 1, and 2, so the
start state is State 3.

The transitions to shift states correspond to shifting a
token out of the on-deck circle into the stack. If the on-deck circle is not occupied, it is loaded from the head of the queue in
order to do the shift. Usually, the next token to be handled is
inspected to see if a shift is what should happen in this circumstance. Because of the way the FSM is designed, all of the
transitions entering any state will shift the same token. An
error is detected by trying to shift a token for which there is no
transition.

Reduce States

The transitions entering the reduce states (squares) correspond
to performing a reduction on the stack top. Reduce states are
entered with only a unique reduce transition and only from a
shift state. They correspond to there being a phrase on the stack
top. The phrase is popped off the stack top. One of the productions will have this phrase as its right part. The left-hand part of
this production is inserted into the on-deck circle. A special
reduce state (double square) is the Halt state.

10.2.2.3. FSM Parser Operation

The stack entries are of the form (q, s), where q is a state of the controller and s is the token shifted to get the FSM into the State q. The
current operational state of the controller is the state in the top entry
of the stack. The pair (q, s) is put on the stack when a shift is done.
In some current operational state, token s was read to get to the next

State q. The State q then becomes the current operational state, and whatever action should happen in that state is done.

If the current state has a transition to a reduce state (a *reduce transition*), nothing is put on the stack and a reduction is done. This entails

(1) popping the RHS of a production (the phrase) off the stack, thus exposing a new current state, and

(2) inserting the LHS of the production in the on-deck circle.

A new current state will be exposed during step (1). Because of the way the parser is constructed, this new state will be a shift state having a shift transition for the non-terminal placed in the on-deck circle during step (2). This shift is done, and parsing proceeds.

Initially the stack contains (q_{start}, ε). The symbol ε represents the empty token; no token was read to enter the start state. Finally the stack contains (q_{start}, ε) and the queue is empty.

Several examples of the parser in Figure 10.3 operating on strings of input tokens appear in the tables below:

Stack	Queue
(q_3, ε)	$aabb\ddagger$
$(q_3, \varepsilon)(q_6, a)$	$abb\ddagger$
$(q_3, \varepsilon)(q_6, a)(q_6, a)$	$bb\ddagger$
$(q_3, \varepsilon)(q_6, a)(q_6, a)(q_9, b)$	$b\ddagger$
$(q_3, \varepsilon)(q_6, a)$	$Sb\ddagger$
$(q_3, \varepsilon)(q_6, a)(q_7, S)$	$b\ddagger$
$(q_3, \varepsilon)(q_6, a)(q_7, S)(q_8, b)$	$\ddagger$
(q_3, ε)	$S\ddagger$
$(q_3, \varepsilon)(q_4, S)$	$\ddagger$
$(q_3, \varepsilon)(q_4, S)(q_5, \ddagger)$	
(q_3, ε)	

Because of the way the FSM is constructed, if a given token is shifted in some state, there will be a unique transition from that state that shifts the token. Also, the FSM is designed so that all of the transitions entering any state will shift the same token. An error is detected by trying to shift a token for which there is no transition. If a reduction is to be done, there will be a deterministic way to determine which reduction and to separate when to do it from when to do any possible shifts. All this means that the tokens in the stack are redundant. The state names will do, and the example should be written as follows:

Stack	Queue
q_3	$aabb\ddagger$
$q_3\, q_6$	$abb\ddagger$
$q_3\, q_6\, q_6$	$bb\ddagger$
$q_3\, q_6\, q_6\, q_9$	$b\ddagger$
$q_3\, q_6$	$Sb\ddagger$
$q_3\, q_6\, q_7$	$b\ddagger$
$q_3\, q_6\, q_7\, q_8$	$\ddagger$
q_3	$S\ddagger$
$q_3\, q_4$	$\ddagger$
$q_3\, q_4\, q_5$	
q_3	

The following example shows the detection of an error. In this example, only the state number has been written. State q_3 is represented as 3.

Stack	Queue
3	$aabab\ddagger$
3 6	$abab\ddagger$
3 6 6	$bab\ddagger$
3 6 6 9	$ab\ddagger$
3 6	$Sab\ddagger$
3 6 7	$ab\ddagger$

The error is detected because there is no read transition for an a in State 7.

The example FSM is deterministic because there is always exactly one thing to do. However, due to the elementary grammar it is simplistic because no lookahead in the input text is required to make it deterministic.

Table 10.1: Augmenting the Grammar.	
Original Production	Augmented Production
$Z \rightarrow S\ddagger$	$Z \rightarrow S\ddagger O_0$
$S \rightarrow aSb$	$S \rightarrow aSb O_1$
$S \rightarrow ab$	$S \rightarrow ab O_2$

Table 10.2: Notation for Augmented Marked Productions.				
Augmented Production	Marked Symbol in Right Part	Index of Marked Symbol	Pictorial Notation	Algebraic Notation
$Z \to S{\ddagger}\bigcirc_0$	S	1	$Z \to \boldsymbol{S} \ddagger \bigcirc_0$	[0,1| S |]
$Z \to S{\ddagger}\bigcirc_0$	‡	2	$Z \to S \ddagger \bigcirc_0$	[0,2| ‡ |]
$Z \to S{\ddagger}\bigcirc_0$	$\bigcirc_0$	3	$Z \to S \ddagger \bullet_0$	[0,3|$\bigcirc_0$|-]
$S \to aSb\bigcirc_1$	a	1	$S \to \boldsymbol{a}\, S\, b\, \bigcirc_1$	[1,1| a |]
$S \to aSb\bigcirc_1$	S	2	$S \to a\, \boldsymbol{S}\, b\, \bigcirc_1$	[1,2| S |]
$S \to aSb\bigcirc_1$	b	3	$S \to a\, S\, \boldsymbol{b}\, \bigcirc_1$	[1,3| b |]
$S \to aSb\bigcirc_1$	$\bigcirc_1$	4	$S \to a\, S\, b\, \bullet_1$	[1,4|$\bigcirc_1$|-]
$S \to ab\bigcirc_2$	a	1	$S \to \boldsymbol{a}\, b\, \bigcirc_2$	[2,1| a |]
$S \to ab\bigcirc_2$	b	2	$S \to a\, \boldsymbol{b}\, \bigcirc_2$	[2,2| b |]
$S \to ab\bigcirc_2$	$\bigcirc_2$	3	$S \to a\, b\, \bullet_2$	[2,3|$\bigcirc_2$|-]

10.2.3. Three Examples

Three examples should serve to show the FSM construction technique sufficiently to permit its use with any arbitrary grammar that it can cope with. The first example is elementary and for an artificial language. No special cases arise with it. This example is followed by a discussion of lookaheads as a way to make some FSM controllers deterministic. The second example shows little but the resolution of a non-deterministic state in a tiny FSM controller. The third example derives a parser for Everybody's Favourite Grammar, from Example 3 of Section 8.2.2.

10.2.3.1. Example One: Basics

The first step in the construction of the controlling algorithm is to augment each production of the grammar. The productions are numbered in sequence with the positive integers. It is conventional to number the goal production as zero.

In the augmented grammar, production k has a $\bigcirc_k$ appended to the end of its right part. This serves to identify the production and to signal the end of the right part. The augmented grammar for Example One is shown in Table 10.1.

Algebraic Notation

20:   $[0,1|\ S\ |21]$ [The S productions should be here.]
21:   $[0,2|\ \ddagger\ |22]$
22:   $[0,3|\circ_0|\!-\!]$ reduce Production 0 = Halt.

Pictorial Notation

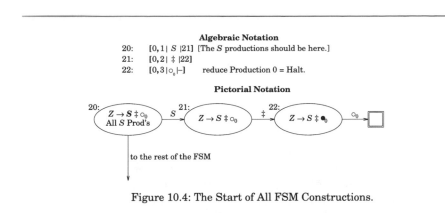

to the rest of the FSM

Figure 10.4: The Start of All FSM Constructions.

The process of generating the controller proceeds in a number of discrete steps. In the description of these steps given below, a narration is included to provide some insight behind the motivation for that step. The basic idea is to assume that the controller will never need to look at the token at the head of the queue in order to be

Algebraic Notation

3:   $[0,1|\ S\ |4]\ [1,1|\ a\ |6]\ [2,1|\ a\ |6]$
4:   $[0,2|\ \ddagger\ |5]$
5:   $[0,3|\circ_0|\!-\!]$ reduce Production 0 = Halt.

Pictorial Notation

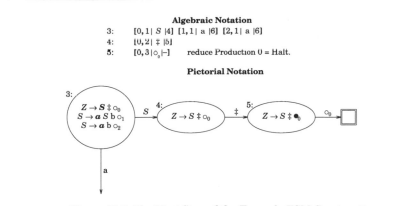

a

Figure 10.5: The First Step of the Example FSM Construction.

deterministic. As we shall see, this is not always the case; sometimes a *lookahead* will need to be added at a local point in the controller to resolve a non-determinism.

Each of the shift and reduce transitions corresponds to a symbol in the right part of one or more augmented productions. The *marked augmented productions* are central to the development that follows. There are a number of tokens in the right part of a production. Any one of these can be *marked*, to correspond to some action in a state. If any but the O_k is marked, this state has a transition to another shift state involving a shift of the marked token. If the O_k is marked, this state has a reduce transition for production k.

There are two complementary notations to describe these productions. The two notations are shown in Table 10.2. Either notation may be used. In the example below both techniques are shown. It is normal to use the pictorial approach when hand-working small examples and to use the algebraic notation for larger examples.

Algebraic Notation

3:	$[0,1\| S \|4]$ $[1,1\| a \|6]$ $[2,1\| a \|6]$
4:	$[0,2\| \ddagger \|5]$
5:	$[0,3\|o_0\|\dashv]$ reduce Production 0 = Halt.
6:	$[1,2\| S \|7]$ $[2,2\| b \|9]$ $[1,1\| a \|6]$ $[2,1\| a \|6]$

Pictorial Notation

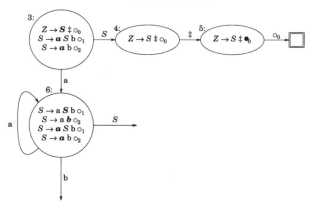

Figure 10.6: The Second Step of the Example FSM Construction.

In the pictorial notation, the marked token in the marked augmented production is shown in a bold font. Since this notation is a part of a picture, the state that is the destination of the transition that shifts the marked token does not explicitly appear in the notation; it is evident from the picture. The transition is drawn in the picture as an arrow, with the designation for the actual token beside it.

In the algebraic notation, the marked augmented production has the form $[p, m | \phi | k]$ in which p is the production number (the subscript in $\bigcirc_p$), m is an index into the right part of the marked augmented production indicating the marked token, ϕ is the actual marked token, and k is the state number of the destination state of the transition that shifts the marked token. If this destination state is not yet known at some stage of the development of the controller, this field is left blank. Marked augmented productions that signify a reduce have no next state. The symbol – is written in the next state field in this case. It isn't strictly necessary to write the shifted token ϕ in this notation, because the marked token is identified by p and m, but it is a great help when working by hand.

The pictorial notation is fine for little grammars, up to about a dozen productions, but falls apart for larger grammars because typically the picture gets too big and unwieldy. The algebraic notation is necessary for larger grammars, and can be used regardless of the number of productions.

Let the highest numbered production be production K. It will prove convenient to start numbering the states from $K+1$. This makes it easy to identify whether a given number is a state name or a production number. Make State $K+1$ the start state, so it can be found easily.

The entire controller is generated from the single marked augmented production $Z \rightarrow S \ddagger \bigcirc_0$. This production is in the start state of every controller. Figure 10.4 shows the beginning of the construction of every controller. For descriptive purposes in Figure 10.4, it has been assumed that there are 20 productions so that the highest numbered production will be 19, and the start state will be State 20. These numbers will change in an obvious way if there are fewer or more productions.

An S production is a production with S as its left part. This prototype controller implies that it is always the case that the sentence (excluding the trailing $\ddagger$) must always be derivable from, or reduce to, an S. The S is that in the goal production, and the states shown are those that (at run time) work the mark across the goal production and finally end up in the halt state. The mark moves one token at a time as tokens are shifted into the stack, until a reduce is done. A reduce

Algebraic Notation

3:      [0,1| S |4] [1,1| a |6] [2,1| a |6]
4:      [0,2| ‡ |5]
5:      [0,3|o_0|⊢]   reduce Production 0 = Halt.
6:      [1,2| S 7|] [2,2| b |9] [1,1| a |6] [2,1| a |6]
7:      [1,3| b |8]
8:      [1,4|o_1|⊢]
9:      [2,3|o_2|⊢]

Pictorial Notation

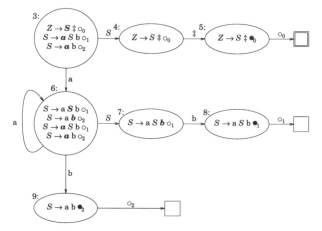

Figure 10.7: The Final Step of the Example FSM Construction.

happens every time an augmenting o_k is marked, revealing the reason for doing the augmentation.

Step 1 of the construction of the controlling FSM is to draw the nucleus as shown above, filling in the S productions. This is shown in Figure 10.5 in both algebraic and pictorial notation. The transition from State 3, shifting an a onto the stack, is taken because of both the marked augmented productions that have a marked. These are the S productions for this grammar. So far, all that is known is that an a is to be shifted; it will be because of either of the marked augmented productions. Further into the machine these paths will diverge, but for the moment they must be combined.

During Step 2 of the example FSM construction, the rest of the states and transitions are filled in, one by one. As seen in Figure 10.6, the next state is the one entered from State 3 shifting an a.

State 6 has the two marked augmented productions that it inherits from State 3 with the mark moved one token to the right, and two marked augmented productions generated because one of these marked augmented productions shifts an 'S', and wherever a non-terminal is shifted, anything that is derivable from the non-terminal can also be shifted. The addition of the last two marked augmented productions to State 6 is caused by this. The process continues with Step 3 shown in Figure 10.7, adding one after the other states 7, 8, and 9, and completing the FSM.

In Step 2, the marked productions that were developed in State 6, and that are associated with reading an a, imply that there should be a state in the machine that has in it these productions with the mark moved one token to the right. Initially, such a state might be generated, but it will be found to be identical to State 6, so the two states are merged. Whenever the destination state for a transition shifting a given token is being generated, the marked augmented productions that must be its *kernel* are those that are imported from the marked augmented productions of the state the transition comes from. They are those marked augmented productions that have that token marked. In the new kernel, the mark is moved one token to the right. This new kernel should be compared with the kernel of all existing states to see if such a state already exists; if one does, the states should be merged. In the case of State 6, failure to merge the states will result in failure of the algorithm. Copies of State 6 will be generated over and over, every time the transition shifting a is developed.

Table 10.3: The Initial FSM Controller.					
	S	a	b	$\ddagger$	Notes
3	4	6			
4				5	
5	0	0	0	0	reduce state
6	7	6	9		
7			8		
8	1	1	1	1	reduce state
9	2	2	2	2	reduce state

This completes the initial development of the FSM controller. There remain some steps to represent the controller in an efficient way. A tabular form with the rows indexed by the current state and the columns indexed by the token at the head of the queue is appropriate. The entries in this next-state table are either the next current state or the number of the production to apply. There is no possibility of confusion because the production numbers are all smaller than the state numbers. The initial table is shown in Table 10.3. The initial FSM can be manipulated into a more convenient form by the following steps:

(1)   State 5 can be removed. There is nothing left of the input text to serve as a column index, so removing State 5 actually makes the FSM easier to work with. Entries in the table that indicate a transition to State 5 are simply changed to a zero to indicate that the goal production should be applied.

(2)   Consider State 9, in which production 2 is applied. Presently, every entry in this row is a 2 to indicate that production 2 should be applied regardless of the next input token. But S can never be an input token (a non-terminal cannot appear in the input text), and in fact a can never occur at this point in a valid sentence. In general, in a reduce state, the grammar should be examined to establish what tokens can legitimately appear at that point; the SLR lookahead algorithm of the next section does exactly that, and the result of using it on states 8 and 9 is shown in Table 10.4.

Table 10.4: The Final FSM Parser.				
	S	a	b	‡	Notes
3	4	6			
4				0	Omit Shifting ‡
6	7	6	9		
7			8		
8			1	1	Lookahead added
9			2	2	Lookahead added

Finally, Table 10.5 shows the length of the right part of the original productions (in tokens). This is needed so the parser will know how many tokens to pop off the stacktop during a reduce operation. The parser also needs to know what non-terminal is the left part of each production; this non-terminal is the one that is moved to the on-deck circle during a reduce.

For a real programming language, the grammar is likely to have 100 or more productions and there will be at least 100 distinct tokens, including both terminals and non-terminals. The next-state Table can become quite large. Fortunately, several sophisticated techniques have been developed to compress the Table to a much smaller size

Table 10.5: The Production Data.		
production number	right part length	left part non-terminal
0	2	Z
1	3	S
2	2	S

without significant added running time cost. Overall, the Tables end up quite small. How small depends on the grammar. The parser will run remarkably rapidly because the entire logic of the algorithm is in the Table.

10.2.3.2. Calculating Lookaheads

Controlling algorithms for FSM deterministic bottom-up parsers have two types of interstate transitions:

Shift Transitions

These shift the leading token of the input text to the stack-top (or shift some equivalent data object) and the destination state becomes a current state.

Reduce Transitions

These rewrite-in-reverse the top of the stack according to a production of the grammar. The right part of the production is popped off the stack, exposing the state in which its first token was read. The left part of the production is added to the front of the input text, becoming a new (additional) leading token. Parsing resumes with the exposed state as the current state.

Lookaheads are of significance only to reduce transitions. The reduction action on the stack-top does not involve in any way the

$$Z \rightarrow E\ddagger\bigcirc_0$$
$$E \rightarrow x + E\bigcirc_1$$
$$E \rightarrow x\bigcirc_2$$

Figure 10.8: A Simple Arithmetic Grammar.

leading token of the input text. However, it is evident that only a subset of all terminal tokens can validly exist at the head of the input text when a reduction is about to be performed, and non-terminals can never appear there. If these input tokens are looked at ahead of doing the reduction, several benefits can be achieved.

(1)   An impending error can be detected before the reduction is done. The advantages of doing this are efficiency and effective reporting.

(2)   The lookahead set of valid next leading tokens for a given reduction might resolve any non-determinism that may exist in a state. A state is said to be non-deterministic when it has two or more transitions to other states and at least one of them involves a reduction. A reduction can not be done simultaneously with anything else. One or the other must be done. Looking further into the input token stream can often resolve which to do in a deterministic way. The lookahead sets for all transitions from a state must be mutually disjoint in order to do this.

There are various FSM-type parsers. They are distinguished from each other solely by the method that is used to compute lookahead sets. The SLR technique develops lookahead sets by an analysis of the grammar. It determines all tokens that can ever validly follow each non-terminal in any sentential form.

It is practical for grammars to permit productions to have empty right parts. It is possible to restructure the grammar so that it never has an empty right part. This simplifies the situation considerably. Grammars that have a few productions with empty right parts, and where the goal production has a terminal as the final token of its

---

3:      $[0,1|\ E\ |7]\ [1,1|\ x\ |4]\ [2,1|\ x\ |4]$

4:      $[1,2|\ +\ |5]\ [2,2|O_2|-]$

5:      $[1,3|\ E\ |6]\ [1,1|\ x\ |4]\ [2,1|\ x\ |4]$

6:      $[1,4|O_1|-]$

7:      $[0,2|\ \ddagger\ |8]$

8:      $[0,3|O_0|-]$

Figure 10.9: The FSM Development for the Simple Grammar.

---

right part (the goalpost), can easily be converted to a grammar
without empty right parts. This must be done before the FSM is constructed.

The procedure to remove productions with empty right parts is
as follows: Assume that $B \rightarrow \varepsilon$ is a production with an empty right
part. For every production with an instance of B in its right part, say
$A \rightarrow \gamma B \delta$, add a new production $A \rightarrow \gamma \delta$ to the grammar. When all
such productions have been added, the production $B \rightarrow \varepsilon$ can be
removed from the grammar. In some cases, some of the productions
added in this way may themselves have empty right parts. These
must also be removed from the grammar in the way just indicated.
Eventually, there will be no productions with empty right parts in the
grammar.

It will be assumed that all productions in the grammar have a
non-empty right part; that is, if the production is $A \rightarrow \beta$, β is not
empty.

The SLR lookahead algorithm starts with the definition of two
functions, *First* and *Follow*, associated with the grammar.

First If A is any non-terminal, let $First(A)$ be the set of terminals that
begin strings derived from A. If a is any terminal, then
$First(a) = a$. Call the set of all productions with A as a left part
the A productions. The A productions will have either a terminal or a non-terminal as the first token of the right part. By

Table 10.6: The Next-State Matrix for the Simple Grammar.

	E	x	+	‡	Notes
3	7	4			
4			5		also reduce 2
5	6	4			
6					reduce 1
7				8	
8					reduce 0

Table 10.7: The Deterministic Next-State Matrix.

	E	x	+	‡	Notes
3	7	4			
4			5	2	Resolved
5	6	4			
6				1	
7				0	

assumption, no right part will be empty. One major component of $First(A)$ is the union of all terminals S_T that are the first token of the right hand part of any A production. Let the set S_N be the set of non-terminals that are the first token of the right hand part of some A production. Then for all $D \in S_N$, $First(A) = First(A) \cup First(D)$. If during this process there develops a case where $C \in First(C)$ for some non-terminal C, it may be deleted from its own $First$ set. It does not invalidate the result, but it will serve no useful purpose.

$$First(A) = [\ S_T \cup \{\ First(D)\ |\ D \in S_N\ \}\ ]$$

These definitions are the basis of an obvious and simple algorithm to compute the $First$ function for all tokens in the grammar. Further elaboration, such as not requiring the deletion of productions with empty right parts, will be left as an exercise.

Follow

If A is non-terminal, define $Follow(A)$ to be the set of terminals that can immediately succeed A in some sentential form. That is, if a is a terminal and $Z \Rightarrow^* \delta A a \gamma$, then $Follow(A)$ contains a. A cannot be the rightmost token in a sentential form because of the assumption that the goal production ends with a terminal. All sentential forms must end with that terminal, too. To compute $Follow(A)$ for all $A \in N$, first set $Follow(A)$ to be the empty set for all A, and then apply the rules below recursively, until nothing can be added to any $Follow$ set.

(1)   If there is a production $B \rightarrow \alpha A \beta$, and β is not empty, then let the first token of β be Y. Then

$$
\begin{aligned}
Z &\rightarrow E \ \ddagger \quad \bigcirc_0 \\
E &\rightarrow E \ + \ T \quad \bigcirc_1 \\
E &\rightarrow T \quad \bigcirc_2 \\
T &\rightarrow P \quad \bigcirc_3 \\
T &\rightarrow P \ \times \ T \quad \bigcirc_4 \\
P &\rightarrow x \quad \bigcirc_5 \\
P &\rightarrow (\ E\ ) \quad \bigcirc_6
\end{aligned}
$$

Figure 10.10: Augmented Everybody's Favourite Grammar.

$$Follow(A) = Follow(A) \cup First(Y) \quad .$$

(2)   If there is a production B →αA, then

$$Follow(A) = Follow(A) \cup Follow(B) \quad .$$

Having determined *Follow*, the SLR lookahead set computation is elementary. If A is the left part of a production, the lookahead set

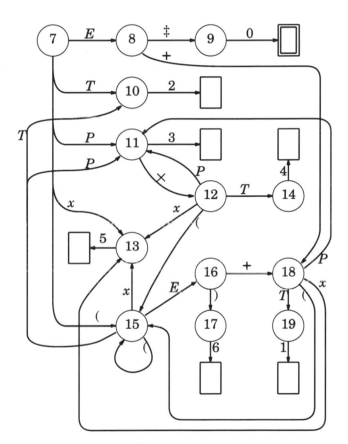

Figure 10.11: Pictorial FSM for Everybody's Favourite Grammar.

for that production is *Follow* (*A*). When a reduction is being done, the right part of the production (the phrase) is in the stacktop, and this is replaced by the left part. The next terminal (the one now in the head of the queue) must be in the lookahead set for the left part of the production (now in the on-deck circle).

Sometimes, the lookahead algorithm cannot resolve the problems with the non-determinant state. This happens when a state has some shift transitions and one or more reduce transitions. The lookahead sets and the set of all shifted tokens must be mutually disjoint if the non-determinacy is to be resolved. If they are not mutually disjoint, either the grammar is not SLR, or it is ambiguous. In either case, the grammar will require modification if this type of parser is to be used.

10.2.3.3. *Example Two: Lookaheads*

As a second example, showing a non-deterministic state for which the non-determinism can be resolved using the SLR lookahead technique,

---

7. $[0,1|\ E\ |8]\ \ [1,1|\ E\ |8]\ \ [2,1|\ T\ |10]\ \ [3,1|\ P\ |11]\ \ [4,1|\ P\ |11]$
      $[5,1|\ x\ |13]\ \ [6,1|\ (\ |15]$
8. $[0,2|\ \ddagger\ |9]\ \ [1,2|\ +\ |18]$
9. $[0,3|O_0|-]$
10. $[2,2|O_2|-]$
11. $[3,2|O_3|-]\ \ [4,2|\ \times\ |12]$
12. $[4,3|\ T\ |14]\ \ [3,1|\ P\ |11]\ \ [4,1|\ P\ |11]\ \ [5,1|\ x\ |13]\ \ [6,1|\ (\ |15]$
13. $[5,2|O_5|-]$
14. $[4,4|O_4|-]$
15. $[6,2|\ E\ |16]\ \ [1,1|\ E\ |8]\ \ [2,1|\ T\ |10]\ \ [3,1|\ P\ |11]\ \ [4,1|\ P\ |11]$
      $[5,1|\ x\ |13]\ \ [6,1|\ (\ |15]$
16. $[6,3|\ )\ |17]\ \ [1,2|\ +\ |18]$
17. $[6,4|O_6|-]$
18. $[1,3|\ T\ |19]\ \ [3,1|\ P\ |11]\ \ [4,1|\ P\ |11]\ \ [5,1|\ x\ |13]\ \ [6,1|\ (\ |15]$
19. $[1,4|O_1|-]$

Figure 10.12: Algebraic FSM for Everybody's Favourite Grammar.

---

consider the (over-simplified) augmented arithmetic grammar shown in Figure 10.8. The parser is developed using the algebraic notation.

The development of the FSM controller for the grammar of Figure 10.8 is shown in Figure 10.9, and the next-state matrix in Table 10.6. Since production 2 is the highest numbered production, the start state is state 3 again. State 4 is non-deterministic because it asks the controller to do both a shift and a reduce. This non-determinism can be resolved by calculating the look aheads by the SLR algorithm.

$$First\,(\ddagger)=\ddagger \qquad Follow\,(Z)=\varepsilon$$
$$First\,(x)=x \qquad Follow\,(E)=\ddagger$$
$$First\,(+)=+$$
$$First\,(E)=x$$
$$First\,(Z)=x$$

In the FSM controller for this grammar, state 4 is non-deterministic, because if the next token is + it must be shifted, but also production 2 is to be applied. Production 2 has E as its left part, and $Follow(E) = \{\ddagger\}$. Consequently the non-determinism can be resolved. If a + is next shift it, but if a $\ddagger$ is next do the reduce. This is shown in Table 10.7. The table of production data is left as an exercise.

The lookahead is used in a very similar way when deciding which tokens can next appear after a reduce is done. The result is evident in the tables. State 6 has an entry in only the $\ddagger$ column, because no other token can follow E, its left part non-terminal.

Table 10.8: The Next-State Matrix for the FSM.

	E	T	P	x	+	×	(	)	$\ddagger$
7	8	10	11	13			15		
8					18				0
10					2			2	2
11					3	12		3	3
12		4	11	5					
13					5			5	5
14					4			4	4
15	16	2	11	5			15		
16					18			6	
17					6			6	6
18		1	11	5			15		
19					1			1	1

Table 10.9: The Production Data for the FSM.

prod'n number	right part length	left part non-terminal	lookahead set
0	2	Z	
1	3	E	$\{ +,), \ddagger \}$
2	1	E	$\{ +,), \ddagger \}$
3	1	T	$\{ +,), \ddagger \}$
4	3	T	$\{ +,), \ddagger \}$
5	1	P	$\{ +, \times,), \ddagger \}$
6	3	P	$\{ +, \times,), \ddagger \}$

10.2.3.4. Example Three: EFG

As a final example, a parser for Everybody's Favourite Grammar is developed. This is substantially more complicated than the previous examples, but it still does not approach the level of complication that happens with real grammars for practical languages. Everybody's Favourite Grammar is about as complicated as it is practical to consider doing by hand. Many more productions and it would pay to write a program to generate the FSM, rather than struggling with the detailed record-keeping that results from the hand work.

The augmented grammar is shown in Figure 10.10. The pictorial version of the controller is in Figure 10.11, without showing the marked augmented productions in the states. The marked augmented productions that should be in each state are easily deduced from the algebraic version of the controller shown in Figure 10.12.

The FSM that has been developed is shown in Table 10.8. State 11 is non-deterministic. This has been resolved with lookaheads. The lookahead sets for the non-terminals in Everybody's Favourite Grammar are shown in Table 10.9 along with the production data.

10.3. TOP-DOWN PARSING

A top down parser uses an arrangement of data and program structures that superficially look very similar to those used by a bottom-up parser. However, the way these objects are used is fundamentally distinct from bottom-up parsing.

The operation of the parser, shown in Figure 10.13, is simple. Initially, the goal is in the stacktop, with a unique symbol (often called the left goalpost) in the second cell in the stack. The queue is filled with the sentence of tokens, so that the first token is at the read head. In some forms of top down parsing, objects other than tokens are put in the stack, but the effect will be the same in principle.

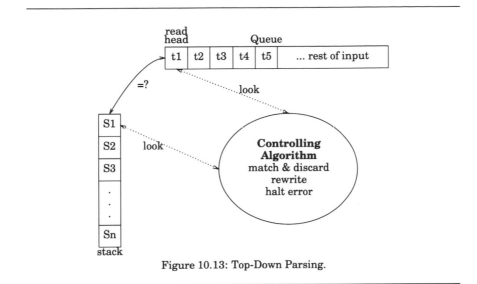

Figure 10.13: Top-Down Parsing.

Assuming that the stack contains tokens, there are four operations that can happen:

Rewrite

If the stacktop token is a non-terminal, say A, the right part of one of the A productions is pushed into the stack, last token first. If the production is $A \rightarrow X_1 X_2 X_3$, first X_3, then X_2, and finally X_1 is pushed into the stack. The method used to choose which A production's right part to use is one of the principle differences between the various top down techniques.

Match and Discard

If the stacktop token is a terminal, and it matches the token at the read head, both tokens are discarded. The stack is popped, discarding the stacktop token, and the tokens in the queue jogged one to the left to give a new token under the read head.

Error

If the stacktop token is a terminal, and it does not match the token at the read head, an error is detected. As in bottom-up parsing, an independent error recovery algorithm is called to permit the parse to continue. Error recovery algorithms are outside the scope of these notes.

Halt Successfully

If the stacktop contains the left goalpost, and the queue is empty, the sentence will have been successfully parsed. Extra input left in the queue when the left goalpost appears in the stacktop is an error.

10.3.1. Recursive Descent

One of the earliest top down parsers, and one of the most common, is the recursive descent type. In a recursive descent parser, the stack exists but is hidden from the programmer. A set of mutually recursive procedures is written, one for each non-terminal, and the stack is the data structure that contains the nested return addresses for each of these procedure calls.

An example will help make the recursive descent technique clearer. Let the grammar be as shown on the left side of Table 10.10. There is no left recursion in this grammar, even though it is obviously related to Everybody's Favourite Grammar. The grammar is rewritten in a related notation as shown on the right side of Table 10.10.

Table 10.8: Recursive Descent Grammar.	
$Z \rightarrow E\ddagger$	$Z \rightarrow E\ddagger$
$E \rightarrow T+E$	$E \rightarrow T\{+T\}$
$E \rightarrow T$	
$T \rightarrow P{\times}T$	$T \rightarrow P\{{\times}P\}$
$T \rightarrow P$	
$P \rightarrow (E)$	$P \rightarrow x \mid (E)$
$P \rightarrow x$	

In this new notation, the meaning of $\{w\}$ is zero or more instances of the string w. We might also have (not in this example) $[w]$ meaning optionally a single instance of w.

This new notation is closely related to the conventional CFG notation. Consider the E productions $E \rightarrow T+E$ and $E \rightarrow T$. The construction of the special grammar form depends on *left factoring* these productions, as shown below. The notation using the square brackets and braces is another way of writing these left factored productions.

$$E \rightarrow TE' \quad E' \rightarrow +E \quad E' \rightarrow$$

This type of transformation is not always convenient.

The read head points at the start of the source program text (the tokens). A suite of mutually recursive procedures, given below, is the core of the parser. To start the parser, the goal procedure (Z) is called. In this example, a valid arithmetic expression is the sentence, and the parser writes out the expression in postfix form. For simplicity, the only identifier is x. When procedure Z returns to its caller, if the variable Success is true, no error has occurred.

```
var Success: boolean              % valid expression?
procedure Z
    import (var Success)
    Success := true           % assume it valid
    E                 % find an expression
    if not Success then return
    if nextInputToken( "‡" )     % look first
    then
        return            % return for valid expression
    else
        Success := false    % extra input text
        return
    end Z

procedure E
    import (var Success)
    T                     % find a term
    if not Success then return
    loop
        exit when not nextInputToken( "+" )
        moveTokenPointer        % space over "+"
        T                 % find another term
        if not Success then return
        put "+"
    end loop
    return
    end E

procedure T
    import (var Success)
    P                     % find a primary
    if not Success then return
    loop
        exit when not nextInputToken( "✕" )
        moveTokenPointer        % space over "✕"
        P             % find another primary
        if not Success then return
        put "✕"
    end loop
    return
    end T

procedure P
    import (var Success)
    if nextInputToken( "x" )                 % look first
```

```
then
    put "x"
    moveTokenPointer          % space over "x"
    return
end if
if nextInputToken( "(" )
then                          % found ( E )
    moveTokenPointer
    E
    if not Success then return
    if nextInputToken( ")" )
    then
        moveTokenPointer
        return
    else
        moveTokenPointer
        Success := false      % missing ")"
    end if
end if
Success := false              % missing primary
return
end P
```

The undefined procedures moveTokenPointer and nextInputToken("token") manage the queue. moveTokenPointer shifts the queue to the left so that the next token is at the read head. nextInputToken("token") returns true if and only if the token at the read head is the same as token passed as a parameter. In a more elaborate case, it would be desirable if the parameter passed by nextInputToken("token") could be a class or set of tokens. If an error is detected, the parser returns with Success = false. In this example, no attempt is made to recover and resume parsing.

The stack contains the return addresses established by the mutually recursive calls. It is not possible to put the right part of the production in the stack, because the stack is not accessible. Instead of putting the right part of the production in the stack, the right part is directly and obviously related to the sequence of statements in each procedure.

These procedures do not need any local variables or parameters. Recursive descent can run quite efficiently, but the procedures are usually hand coded and consequently are difficult to change. With local variables and parameters the method is capable of handling any grammar the bottom-up techniques can handle.

10.3.2. Left Recursion

Left recursion is a problem with all top down parsers. In most types of top down parser, left recursion can be added to the capability of the parser with some elaboration like the local variables and parameters in recursive descent. The reason left recursion is a general problem is shown easily. Consider a production $S \rightarrow Sa$. There will be a procedure s, and the first thing that this procedure will do is to call itself, because the right part of the production begins with an S. This will never end. Special actions that consume a token of the input text each time the call is done must be incorporated in the parser if left recursion is present.

To cope with a left recursive grammar, it must be changed. For instance, instead of the left recursive productions $S \rightarrow Sa$ and $S \rightarrow b$, the productions $S \rightarrow bS'$, $S' \rightarrow aS'$, and $S' \rightarrow$ can be used. This transformation may make the grammar into one that can be parsed top down. After the transformation, the left recursion has been replaced with right recursion. There is, however, no guarantee that this will heve the desired result, because other productions in the grammar may interfere with the attempted transformation.

10.4. EXERCISES

1. Develop an SLR controlling algorithm for Everybody's Favorite Grammar, modified to include a prefix negation operator and a raise-to-power operator.
2. By following the principles of Everybody's Favorite Grammar, develop a grammar and a SLR parser for Boolean expressions including the *and*, *or*, and *not* operators. Be sure to get the precedence of the operators correct.
3. Change the grammar developed in Exercise 2 so that a recursive descent parser can be constructed, and write the recursive descent parser.
4. Compare the two parsers that you have built in Exercises 2 and 3. Which was easier to develop? Which is the more easily used by a program? Parse a few sentences to see which you consider to be more convenient to use. Which will make the job of writing the rest of the compiler easier?

A PROGRESSIONS

A.1. PROGRESSIONS

The following two progressions arise frequently in the analysis of algorithms.

Arithmetic Progression

a is the first term, l is the last term, and d is the common difference. If there are n terms, then $l = a + (n-1)d$. The sum A of the progression is

$$A = \sum_{i=0}^{n-1}(a+id) = \frac{n}{2}\left(2a + (n-1)d\right) = \frac{n}{2}\left(a+l\right) \ .$$

Geometric Progression

a is the first term, l is the last term, and r is the common ratio. If there are n terms, then $l = a\,r^{n-1}$. The sum A of the progression is

$$A = \sum_{i=0}^{n-1}(a\,r^{i}) = a\,\frac{1-r^{n}}{1-r} = \frac{a-lr}{1-r} \ .$$

B THE GREEK ALPHABET

It is convenient to use Greek letters to represent many quantities in mathematical work. Since the demise of classics as a subject in the school system, many people do not have a good grasp of the greek alphabet. A list of the letters in this alphabet is given below. Several English letters correspond to more than one Greek letter. This occurs when there is more than one way to pronounce the English letter.

Greek Letter	Greek Name	English Equivalent	Greek Letter	Greek Name	English Equivalent
A α	Alpha	a	N ν	Nu	n
B β	Beta	b	Ξ ξ	Xi	x
Γ γ	Gamma	g	O o	Omicron	o
Δ δ	Delta	d	Π π	Pi	p
E ε	Epsilon	e	P ρ	Rho	r
Z ζ	Zeta	z	Σ σ	Sigma	s
H η	Eta	e	T τ	Tau	t
Θ θ	Theta	th	Y υ	Upsilon	u
I ι	Iota	i	Φ φ	Phi	ph
K κ	Kappa	k	X χ	Chi	ch
Λ λ	Lambda	l	Ψ ψ	Psi	ps
M μ	Mu	m	Ω ω	Omega	o

C
NOTES
TO THE
EXERCISES

C.1. NOTES TO THE EXERCISES
These notes divide the exercises into three groups.

Drill and Practice
> There should be no mystery or difficulty in handling these exercises. They consist mostly of drill in notation or the straightforward application of parts of the text. Students should not avoid doing these exercises. They provide a basic skill level that it is not possible to obtain other than by actual work.

Programming
> There are a few programming exercises included in the text. They are easy and relate directly to the text or to simple extensions of it. Given reasonable facilities they should not cause a problem.

Intellectually Challenging
> We give some hints or advice for these somewhat more challenging exercises.

C.2. CHAPTER 2

C.2.1. Drill Problems
> None.

C.2.2. Programming Problems
5. This exercise is an instance of the type of problem introduced in section 2.1.2.

C.2.3. Challenging Problems

1. This matrix multiply problem is a classic. Every student should be able to work out that it has complexity $O(n^3)$.

2. Assume that the data is to be put in ascending order. For the linear search, the best and worst cases are established by the order that the data is originally in. Assume that the program starts a linear search from element j of the array, working towards element 1. For data that is already in sorted order it will take a constant time (a comparison with element j) to determine that element $j+1$ is already in the proper place. No data needs to be moved. In this case, the sort is $O(n)$ because n elements must be checked to see that they are in the proper order.

    The worst case is when the data is in exactly the improper order. Then there will be j comparisons in each search, each followed by j swaps of elements as the j previous members of the sorted part of the array ripple one position up the array so element $j+1$ can be placed in element 1. The sort is $O(n^2)$.

    A binary search of j elements takes a time $O(\log j)$, so the binary best case is worse than the linear best case. The binary best case works out to be

$$O\left[\sum_{j=2}^{n}\log j\right] = O(\log n\,!) \approx O(n\log n)$$

    searches, and this is worse than the linear case. Like the linear best case, in the binary best case there are no swaps of data.

    The binary worst case entails, for each element $j+1$, an $O(\log j)$ search followed by an $O(j)$ group of swaps to insert element $j+1$ at array element 1 and to ripple the other elements up the sorted part of the array. This means that element $j+1$ takes $O(j + \log j)$, and the sum of this over all elements shows the worst case sort to be $O(n^2)$. Obviously the linear case is the faster, simpler, and preferred insertion sort.

3. The arrays can be merged in one sorted array with complexity $O(n)$, by selecting the smallest not yet selected from the left end of each and moving it to a new array. The median of the new array can be selected easily; it is in element n.

    To do this without merging the arrays, identify A_{mid}, the element at the mid-point of A. Locate B_{mid}, the element near mid-point of B, such that the number of elements in the upper half of B is the same as the number of elements in the lower half of A. Compare A_{mid} and B_{mid}. If $A_{mid} < B_{mid}$ the median must lie somewhere in the upper part of A or the lower part of B.

There are an equal number of elements in the lower part of A and the upper part of B (by construction) and these elements can be ignored because the median must lie between A_{mid} and B_{mid}. If $A_{mid} \geq B_{mid}$ the median must lie somewhere in the lower part of B or the upper part of A, where these parts include A_{mid} and B_{mid}.

Recursively repeat the halving and the comparison of the midpoints on the selected halves of A and B, until there are only one or two elements in each array and the median can be located by direct computation.

Half the array is discarded for each comparison. The number of times that this must be done is the number of times that n objects can be divided in two before there are only 1 or 2 objects left. Starting with n objects, there will be successively

$$n, \frac{n}{2}, \frac{n}{2^2}, \frac{n}{2^3}, \frac{n}{2^4}, \ldots, \frac{n}{2^k}$$

objects in each list. The division stops when the last term of this sequence equals 1. This will take $k+1$ steps, where $k = \log_2 n$. The program complexity is $O(\log_2 n)$.

4.   Because the integer represents a power to which the base is to be raised, and that raise to power can be done without having successive integers being the same.

C.3. CHAPTER 3

C.3.1. Drill Problems
Questions 1, 2, 4, 5, 6.

C.3.2. Programming Problems
None.

C.3.3. Challenging Problems
3.   The divide and conquer approach is no winner. It handles each element in the array once, comparing it with another, and then the biggest with another, etc., for $O(n)$ comparisons. All this and the overhead of the recursive calls. No, thanks.

7.   The worst case of quicksort becomes highly improbable because it would indeed be a fluke if the selected element was one of the extreme elements of the (sub)array at every selection. Let the array have n elements. Let the array be composed of the integers $1..n$. At the start each integer is equally probable to be selected. The array will divide into the selected element ξ and two parts

$1..\xi-1$ and $\xi+1..n$ with probability $1/n$ for each ξ in the interval $1..n$.

The probability of each subarray's divisions can then be worked out, until each subarray has one or no elements. The rest of the problem is left as an exercise.

8. A hint is given in the question. The idea is to try to get the amount of multiplying of polynomials down by replacing it with adding.

Let f and g be polynomials in t of order n. Form f_{lo} from all terms of f up to but not including that with $t^{n/2}$. Form f_{hi} from all terms of f involving powers of t equal to or higher than $n/2$, with the exponent decreased by $n/2$. Then $f = f_{lo} + f_{hi} \times t^{n/2}$. Form g_{lo} and g_{hi} similarly. Then

$$f \times g = f_{lo} \times g_{lo} + (f_{hi} \times g_{lo} + f_{lo} \times g_{hi}) \times t^{n/2} + f_{hi} \times g_{hi} \times t^{n} \quad .$$

So far this saves nothing, because there is still a lot of multiplying. The idea is to calculate $r_{lo} = f_{lo} \times g_{lo}$, $r_{hi} = f_{hi} \times g_{hi}$, and $r_{mi} = (f_{lo} + f_{hi}) \times (g_{lo} + g_{hi})$. Then

$$f \times g = r_{lo} + (r_{mi} - r_{lo} - r_{hi}) \times t^{n/2} + r_{hi} \times t^{n}$$

The $\times t^{n}$ type terms do not actually involve any explicit multiplication, but rather they adjust the terms of the product that the coefficients are added into. Thus, instead of four multiplications, there are three, as the r's are calculated.

The process can be continued recursively on the upper and lower halves of f and g, until the polynimials are of trivial order. It is a simple matter to set up and solve the recursion that this process represents. This approach is pure divide and conquer, with $a=3$ and $c=2$. The complexity is $O(n^{\log_2 3})$.

9. The answer to this question is really too complicated to spend much time on the general case. The answer is that, if $x > y$, then very approximately gcd is $O(\log y)$. Try setting up some instances where x is a power of some integer, and y is chosen as a number less than x. What happens if y is a power of the same integer? What happens if y has the same integer as a factor? as a repeated factor? What happens if x and y have no common factors? What are the probabilities of these things?

C.4. CHAPTER 4

C.4.1. Drill Problems
Questions 1 to 11, 13.

C.4.2. Programming Problems
Questions 12, 16.

C.4.3. Challenging Problems
14. Three bytes have 24 bits, and $2^{24} > 16$ million. Thus, 14289238 records need a three byte pointer, and since there are eight decimal digits in the number of records, probably at least eight bytes of key. Assume that these numbers are the case. Then each record has $8+3j$ bytes minimum. If we use all 2^{19} bytes of memory to hold one node, it can reference $j = 174760$ (sub)nodes. A root node and one full layer of such nodes can reference $174760^2 > 3 \times 10^{10}$ nodes. Any record could be found in two node probes. There is enough data given to infer an approximate time that this would take and to work out the time for nodes with smaller j for comparison.

15. In the j-ary tree, for each parent-sibling family group start with the parent as the root. Connect a left pointer to the eldest sibling, and chain the siblings in age order down a right vine. Repeat recursively for children of the siblings.

C.5. CHAPTER 5

C.5.1. Drill Problems
Questions 1, 3.

C.5.2. Programming Problems
4. Assume the new elements are ordered. (Don't expect miracles!)

C.5.3. Challenging Problems
2. This particular choice of hash function has a remarkably short period. Try making modest changes to the constants 317 or 709 and watch what happens.

C.6. CHAPTER 6

C.6.1. Drill Problems
Questions 1, 2, 4.

C.6.2. Programming Problems
None.

C.6.3. Challenging Problems

3. Disarrange the board by moving tiles about. Now, following a
    regular route, say row by row, work out whether the rows are
    "even" or "odd". An even row has an even number of increases in
    value as it is scanned. An odd row has an odd number of
    increases in value as it is scanned. Look for a pattern. Now, try
    the same thing with an illegal arrangement — an arrangement
    that cannot be arrived at by moving tiles about legitimately. Try-
    ing to solve a Game of 15 puzzle where some twit has put the
    puzzle in the goal position and then swapped the 14 and 15 by
    brute force, often with a prybar, is exasperating. The arrange-
    ment is unreachable from the solution, and the solution is
    unreachable from the arrangement.

5. The formula is $(x_1 + x_2)(\bar{x}_1 + \bar{x}_2)(x_1 + \bar{x}_2)$. The rest is mechanical.

C.7. CHAPTER 7

C.7.1. Drill Problems
Question 1.

C.7.2. Programming Problems
None.

C.7.3. Challenging Problems

2. The repeated calls to "confusion" caused by references to the first
    formal parameter are confusing. In the first call, the formal
    parameter "P" is a reference to the thunk "confusion(BigDeal,
    Three)", and "Q" is a reference to the variable "F". In the state-
    ment "Q := P+Q", the references to "P" cause another call to con-
    fusion with "P" a reference to the variable "BigDeal" and "Q" to
    "Three". The statement causes "Four" to change its value to 21,
    and along the way "Three" changes its value to 10.

    The statement "result P+Q" causes another spate of calls to
    confusion because it again refers to "P". Finally, "Arcane" has the
    value 45.

C.8. CHAPTER 8

C.8.1. Drill Problems
Questions 1, 2, 4, 5, 6, 7, 8, 11.

C.8.2. Programming Problems
None.

C.8.3. Challenging Problems
3. A reference to an array element is done with a syntax obtained from adding productions like the following to the EFG:

$$P \rightarrow x\,(\,L\,)$$
$$L \rightarrow L\,,\,E$$
$$L \rightarrow E \quad .$$

An array reference is the name of the array, followed by a parenthesized list L of indexes. The list L is a comma-separated list of individual row, column, etc., indexes. Each individual index can be an expression. Negation is easily done in several ways. One way is to add to the grammar the productions $P \rightarrow -x$ and $P \rightarrow -(\,E\,)$. Exponentiation requires the addition of a right recursive pair of productions of the form $F \rightarrow P ** F$ and $F \rightarrow P$. The F replaces the P in the T productions. The tricky bit is to do these last two additions so that their combination results in the desired effect. This is left for the student.

9. Right or left recursion being preferable depends upon the semantics of the phrase. Syntactically, they can result in the same language and either can be used. For instance, with exponentiation it is natural to use right recursion because the phrases will be recognized in the proper order for generating fragments of code. $a**b**c$ means $a**(b**c)$. But adding and subtracting are conventionally thought of as left recursive. Sometimes, it is not clear what is actually meant by an expression. Some people think $a/b/c$ means $a/(b*c)$, while others think it means $a/(b/c)$. The former is intrinsically connected with left recursion, the latter with right recursion. Choose one and emphatically assert it to be correct.

10. $G_1 = ab^+a\ddagger;\ G_2 = ab^+ba\ddagger;\ G_3 = ab^+a\ddagger;\ G_4 = ab^+a\ddagger.$

C.9. CHAPTER 9
Chapter 9 has no exercises.

C.10. CHAPTER 10

C.10.1. Drill Problems
Questions 1, 2, 3.

C.10.2. Programming Problems
None.

C.10.3. Challenging Problems
4.   The top-down parser is much easier to develop. Both are easily integrated into a program, but the program that uses the bottom-up approach needs to know little or nothing about the details of the grammar. They are stored in the tables. The top-down may not have this advantage, and so the resulting program may be more difficult to maintain. Bottom-up can handle more types of constructs, like left recursion, than the top-down can. It can recognize the phrases in a more convenient sequence.

Usually, top-down is used for hand-coded parsers for small grammars. Bottom-up for is used for larger grammars, and the tables are often developed by a program called a parser generator. This program accepts the grammar as input and gives the tables as its output. It is easy but tedious to write such a parser generator.

BIBLIOGRAPHY

Any good computer science library will include quite a few references that are relevant to the material in this book. Few of these references will take the viewpoint of the computer engineer. Nevertheless, they are the source of most of the material that has been adapted to appear in this book.

The algorithms and data structures material that appears in this book is well covered by two standard references. Both should be available in every good computer science library. Both include far more material than could be included here.

The first algorithms and data structures reference is Donald E. Knuth, *The Art of Computer Programming*, Reading, Mass., Addison-Wesley, 1973. This three volume set is an admirable and distinguished work of scholarship. It is an excellent and detailed tour through most that was known about algorithms and data structures at the time it was written. There are many example programs, but they are often machine language programs for a fictitious computer. An extensive set of exercises with their solutions is provided.

The second algorithms and data structures reference is Niklaus Wirth, *Algorithms and Data Structures*, Englewood Cliffs, New Jersey, Prentice-Hall, 1986. Wirth's book covers some of the same material that Knuth does, but without most of the formal analysis and in much less detail. It is a particularly readable exposition of the material it covers. Wirth also includes many example programs in his book.

The material on exhaustive searching is elementary and is available in any book that introduces the subject. An example is Ellis Horowitz and Sartaj Sahni, *The Fundamentals of Computer Algorithms*, Potomac, Maryland, Computer Science Press, 1978. By browsing in a library, the reader can easily discover that exhaustive searching is a discipline by itself.

The material covering formal languages and parsers in the last three chapters of this book is drawn from many sources, some of which are unpublished. Perhaps the best single source for further reading is Alfred V. Aho and Jeffrey D. Ullman, *Principles of Compiler Design*, Reading, Mass., Addison-Wesley, 1977. Aho and Ullman have written other books in the area. All are worthwhile.

If mystified or perplexed, the student is encouraged to forage through the appropriate shelves in a good computer science library. The original source of much of computer science is contained in conference proceedings and journals that are not easy to find, and often very difficult to read and understand. Fortunately, computer scientists are prolific writers of textbooks, so most of the important ideas have been interpreted and presented in more findable and palatable form.

INDEX